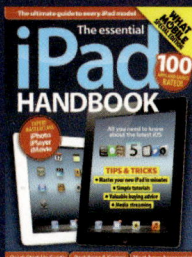

The Essential iPad Handbook

EDITOR
Richard Melville

ART DIRECTOR
Paul Godfrey

PRODUCTION EDITOR
James Nixon

CONTRIBUTORS
Andy Penfold
Rob Buckley
Howard Calvert
Rob Clymo
Fred Dutton
Jonny Evans
Penny Glen
Ben Harvell
Cliff Joseph
Stuart Dredge
Sam Kieldsen
Andrew Brown

PUBLISHING DIRECTOR
Ian White

MANAGING DIRECTOR
Azad Kanani

A WHAT MOBILE PUBLICATION
www.whatmobile.net
Clark White Publishing
Limited, 70-74 City Road
London, EC1Y 2BJ
Registered in England
No. 4671311

PRINTED BY
Precision Colour Printing

DISTRIBUTION
UK, Eire & Rest Of The World:

Intermedia Brand
Marketing Ltd
+44 1737 862166
Email: getintouch@
inter-media.co.uk

Marketforce (UK) Ltd
+44 203 148 3300
Email: mfcommunications@
marketforce.co.uk

ISBN 978-0-9572601-0-8

Welcome…
to The Essential iPad Handbook

The excitement of buying an iPad happens the moment you take it home and open the box. The new iPad reveals a world of new apps, features and games that make the most of the new Retina display, enhanced processor and upgraded camera. Whether you own a new iPad or a previous model, this book will help you get the very best from your iPad and guide you, step by step, through the iOS user interface and key apps like iMovie, BBC iPlayer and iPhoto. Once you've mastered the basics, there's a new level of tips and tricks that will save you time, teach you new skills and help you get even more out of your iPad. Whether you want help with photo-editing, making your music wireless or simply getting emails on your iPad in minutes, we've got a guide for all of these tasks and many, many more. Excited? You should be – there's a world of iPad knowledge in this book and it starts on the next page...

Richard Melville
Editor

Contents

Introduction

✅ *Updated for the new iPad*

Get to know your iPad

Start up

Tutorials to help you master essential iPad features

74

Shopping

✓ *Updated for the new iPad*

The best apps, games and accessories

94

82

Apps in depth ✓ *Updated for the new iPad*

Detailed tutorials show you how to master the best apps

158

Welcome to the...
new iPad

With a stunning display and more processing power than its two predecessors, Apple's new iPad proves third time is luckier than ever. Here's why...

The new iPad is an evolution of everything Apple has strived for since the launch of the original iPad in 2010. In just two years, the pace of technology and innovation has combined to make the new iPad the benchmark for all tablets to follow. Whether you want to browse the web, watch movies or explore thousands of innovative apps that change the way you work and play, the new iPad is a device accessible to everyone and brimming with the kind of innovation and polish that has seen Apple become the technology giant it is today.

What's new?

1. Retina display

The quest for a true HD screen has now been realised via a technology that Apple calls Retina display. If you have an iPhone 4, you'll be familiar with this style of display, but watching a movie or viewing a website on the new iPad is a revelation. The 2048 x 1536 pixel display may sound baffling to some but it's the technology that delivers the ultra-crisp 264 pixels per inch display. In jargon-free terms, that's a higher resolution than high-definition TV and a major step forward if you like watching TV and movies on your iPad. It's a landmark moment for games too, many of which are being enhanced for the new screen. Colours are more vibrant and you won't see any vague blur or pixelation when you zoom in on images or text. If you've used an iPad before, you'll be able to compare the difference by viewing any web page with text, as well as Google Maps or any high-resolution photos you have stored in your iCloud account.

2. A5X processor

The new iPad's A5X chip is a follow-up to the original A5 chip found in the iPad 2. The already impressive processor enhances any graphics you see on the iPad screen, which means that everything from games to image editing functions are faster. Primarily designed to enhance

the growing games market on iPad, the gap between what you see on your TV at home via dedicated games consoles and what the new iPad can provide is rapidly becoming smaller. Importantly for Apple, it raises the bar for rival tablets hoping to score points by offering new processors or graphic chips.

3. iSight camera

The iPad 2's camera was fine for video but always struggled to reach the kind of quality your iPhone can provide. The new iPad's iSight camera is a great step forward for several reasons. It's a

5-megapixel camera and, like the one in the iPhone 4, has an enhanced lens and autofocus functions to really show off the quality of still shots. The latest version of iPhoto is available on the new iPad and makes editing the higher resolution images quick and easy. In addition, the iSight camera delivers enhanced Full HD video – 1080p, instead of the iPad 2's 720p resolution.

4. Wireless technology

The wireless technology inside the new iPad varies, depending on whether you've purchased the WiFi or WiFi

New iPad, new Apple TV

While the new iPad is great for movies and TV, Apple has released a new version of Apple TV to join the debut of the new iPad. Why? The new iPad can now handle full HD 1080p video thanks to its new Retina display and since iTunes movies now come in that format, it's only natural that Apple should want

to upgrade its £99 Apple TV device for iTunes purchased on your TV.

Simply hook up the pocket-sized set-top box to your HD TV and you can stream movies and music from iTunes and rent the latest films. Using your new iPad (or iPhone) as a remote, you can browse services such as Netflix

and Flickr and throw your new iPad picture to the big screen – great for playing games and showing anything visual to friends and family. Apple TV features AirPlay too, so it really is a clever solution for your lounge if you want your iTunes content accessible everywhere.

Watching a movie or viewing a website on the new iPad is a revelation

The new iPad's homescreen offers a few clues about what new software and hardware the gadget packs inside.

New iPad apps

The launch of the new iPad means that many apps have been updated for the new format. The three key offerings from Apple include new iPad exclusive versions of iPhoto (p132), Garageband (p108) and iMovie (p136), all enhanced to take advantage of the new Retina display.

+ 4G version but both models are enhanced in terms of their connectivity options.

The standard WiFi version has been upgraded with the latest Bluetooth 4.0 technology, compared to Bluetooth 2.1 on the iPad 2. The 4G version of the new iPad naturally embraces faster 4G functions but it's a high-speed data streaming standard that hasn't yet reached the UK. The enhanced 4G LTE functions are for use on American mobile networks so you'll need to be in the US with a US network to take advantage of them.

Bluetooth 4.0 technology works in the UK, though, and it's compatible with older forms of Bluetooth streaming technology. What does it do? Bluetooth 4.0 is for use in future fitness gadgets and wireless payment transactions. Expect to see the young format begin to appear on new devices during 2012.

5. Bigger battery

The battery life of phones and tablets is one of the biggest struggles consumers have with new technology. The actual issue surrounding battery life isn't the size of the battery, it's the heat tat's kicked out by a bigger battery before the internal chips and circuitry demand a fan to cool things down. The new iPad doesn't feature a fan of course but does feature a better battery – 42.4 Watt hours (Wh) against a 25Wh battery inside the iPad 2. So, that's nearly double the battery life then? Not quite. The new iPad has a high resolution screen and a better A5X processor which demand power than before. You can still expect a world-class 10-hour battery life from the new iPad, however, which is far ahead of any rival tablets and would make the average laptop or netbook wince.

The new iPad's battery life would make the average laptop or netbook wince

Should you upgrade?

When the iPad 2 arrived, the original iPad was withdrawn from the market. With the launch of the new iPad, Apple has continued to sell iPad 2 at the reduced price of £329.

The two main benefits of the new iPad revolve around its Retina display and the enhanced connectivity options of the 4G version. If you value photos and movies or use your iPad as an eBook reader or browser, the new screen cannot be praised enough and it's hard to go back once you've experienced the difference.

Hot and heavy?

The new iPad is 61g heavier than the iPad 2 but it's actually lighter than the first-generation iPad, so hardcore Apple fans are unlikely to spot the difference. Early reports suggest that

the new iPad gets hotter during use than previous models. This is to be expected given the bigger battery and the power demands of the new processor, and only happens after hours of continuous use. By comparison, the new iPad is still half the weight of a new laptop and is silent thanks to clever design that negates the need for an internal fan.

If you purchase bigger apps, games and HD movies it's likely you'll need more space

The iPad 2 price drop means the resale value of your iPad 2 is likely to be less than you might have expected. The average eBay price for a used 16GB iPad 2 is around £250 which means you'll need roughly £170 to upgrade, after eBay fees have been added to your sale. Is it worth it? Yes – and even if you don't sell your iPad 2, there's the option of passing it to another family member or using it as a second TV, family games console

or a music and movies hub in your lounge using an AV Adapter.

Storage and extra memory options

The new iPad comes in 16GB, 32GB and 64GB models. A gigabyte (GB) is a thousand megabytes (MB) of data.

Typically, an HD movie uses 3GB of data storage while an app like Keynote is just 61MB. 1GB also holds eight albums or a couple of high-end, console-style games.

The new iPad offers identical storage options to the iPad 2, so if you purchase bigger apps, games and HD movies it's likely you'll need more space. The enhanced 5-megapixel camera means file sizes for photos and videos are bigger, too.

64GB is the premium model but if you do need more space, Apple's iCloud wireless storage service (p72) offers upgrade options over the free 5GB iCloud online allowance. 10GB of iCloud storage costs £14 per year, 20GB is £28 per year and 50GB is £70 per year.

If you're don't fancy iCloud or need more space, there's a handy gadget from Seagate can solve the problem too. The GoFlex Satellite is a £179 500GB wireless hard drive that streams content to and from your iPad. The drive is roughly the size of two iPhones and is rechargeable, so you can take it with you and wirelessly access content from your bag when you're out. Better still, multiple users can access the device, so you can all watch the same film or download files, making the GoFlex Satellite an ideal storage option if you use an iPad and don't own a home computer.

The bottom line is that you'll need to use iCloud or an external hard drive if you're planning to watch lots of HD films or download big apps on a 16GB new iPad.

Seagate's 500GB GoFlex Satellite portable wireless hard drive lets you stream content to your iPad while you're on the move.

25 billions apps downloaded

The App store hit 25 billion downloads in March 2012. "We'd like to thank our customers and developers for helping us achieve this historic milestone of 25 billion apps downloaded," said Eddy Cue, Apple's senior vice president of Internet Software and Services. "When we launched the App Store less than four years ago, we never imagined that mobile apps would become the phenomenon they have, or that developers would create such an incredible selection of apps for iOS users."

To date, there are 170,000 native iPad apps available, bringing the combined iPad and iPhone app count to a staggering 550,000.

Chunli Fu of Qingdao, China was the person who downloaded the app that brought Apple to its magic 25 billion mark on March 3rd 2012. Chunli Fu won a $10,000 iTunes gift card – more than enough to cover the purchase of the original app Where's My Water...

SPECS IN DEPTH

Size	242.1 x 185.7 x 9.4mm
Weight	652g 662g
Screen	9.7-inch LED-backlit widescreen Multi-Touch Retina display 2,048 x 1536 pixels at 264ppi
Rear camera	Video: HD (1080p) up to 30fps with audio Stills: 5.0mp with 5x digital zoom
Front camera	Video recording: VGA (30fps) video Stills shooting: 0.3pm
Battery	Built-in 42.5-watt rechargeable lithium-polymer battery
Battery life	10 hours watching video or surfing the web 9 hours web browsing over 3G on WiFi + 4G model
Connectivity	802.11a/b/g/n WiFi Bluetooth 4.0 + EDR technology 4G LTE (700, 2100 MHz); UMTS/ HSPA/HSPA+/DC-HSDPA (850, 900, 1900, 2100 MHz); GSM/EDGE (850, 900, 1800, 1900 MHz)
Processor	Dual-core Apple A5X
RAM	1GB
Sensors	Three-axis gyro, accelerometer, ambient light sensor
Input/output	3.5mm headphone jack 30-pin dock connector Built-in speaker Microphone
Location	WiFi and digital compass Assisted GPS Cellular
Audio	Frequency response: 20Hz-20,000Hz
Audio supported	HE-AAC (V1 and V2), AAC (8- 320Kbps), Protected AAC (from iTunes Store), MP3 (8-320Kbps), MP3 VBR, Audible (formats 2, 3, and 4, Audible Enhanced Audio, AAX, and AAX+), Apple Lossless, AIFF, WAV, Dolby Digital 5.1 surround sound pass-through with Apple Digital AV Adapter
Video	Video-out support up to 1080p with Apple Digital AV Adapter or Apple VGA Adapter
Video supported	H.264 up to 720p, 30fps, Main Profile level 3.1 with AAC-LC audio up to 160Kbps, 48kHz, stereo audio in .m4v, .mp4, and .mov file formats; MPEG-4 video, up to 2.5Mbps, 640 x 480 pixels, 30fps, Simple Profile with AAC-LC audio up to 160 Kbps per channel, 48kHz, stereo audio in .m4v, .mp4, and .mov file formats; Motion JPEG (M-JPEG) up to 35Mbps, 1280 x 720 pixels, 30, audio in ulaw, PCM stereo audio in .avi file format

Items marked in red apply only to the WiFi + 4G models

SUPER SCREEN

The new 9.7-inch screen is four times as sharp as its predecessor, at an astonishing 2048 x 1536 pixel resolution. That's sharper than your TV, your phone, probably even your desktop PC monitor, and why Apple is dubbing it a 'Retina display'. But it's not all stats: the difference is incredible, and makes reading iBooks or watching HD movies from iTunes a real joy.

BIGGER BATTERY

At 9.4mm, the new iPad is just 0.6mm thicker than the razor-thin iPad 2 and yet the battery capacity is almost double. Apple has squeezed in a 42.5Wh battery inside, compared to 25Wh inside the iPad 2. Of course, much of that is being used to push all those extra pixels, but you still get the same impressive ten hours of surfing time.

CAMERA UPGRADE

Apple made it quite clear that the iPad 2 cameras were built for video chats, but the five-megapixel sensor on the back of the new iPad is so good, Apple's given it the iSight branding as used on iPhone 4. The front-facing camera meanwhile lets you carry out smooth FaceTime video chats at VGA resolution.

WAIST ADJUSTMENT

At 241.2 x 185.7 x 9.4 mm, the new iPad has gotten ever so slightly thicker, but you'd be hard pressed to notice thanks to the mesmerising display. It's still thin enough to carry around in your backpack – and light enough too, at just 652g. The 4G version weighs an extra 10g, but you won't notice.

TURBO PROCESSOR

The A5X chip inside the new iPad is a 1GHz dual-core processor with a trick up its sleeve. It also packs a quad-core GPU (Graphics processing unit), which can be used to offload all sorts of tasks. The upshot? Everything is buttery smooth and 3D games such as Infinity Blade can make full and glorious use of all those extra new pixels.

Wireless world

Apple's AirPlay technology brings wireless entertainment home…

Apple is something of a stickler for neat and tidy design. Whether it's removing as many buttons as possible from the iPad, or hiding the iMac's power switch so that most people have to ask where it is, minimalism is key.

So perhaps it's no surprise that Apple is leading the way when it comes to removing wires from the gadget user's life. Wireless technology is novel, convenient, and neat – and it's fast becoming the default feature for all kinds of devices.

Indeed, for gadgets such as the iPad, the ability to connect to the Internet is pivotal, allowing you to access information and communicate on the go. But Apple has moved on to wireless content delivery with technologies such as AirPrint and AirPlay, which could change the way we consume music and video in our homes.

With nothing more than your iPad and a couple of add-on devices, you can effortlessly stream music and video content throughout your house.

Into the stream

Wireless streaming systems for music have been around for a while – for example, those that use Bluetooth. However, quality does suffer when you stream music over Bluetooth, even over A2DP stereo. Some companies have developed proprietary wireless streaming systems, but these usually require you to plug a dongle into your iPad or iPhone. Apple's AirPlay technology does away with all of that, simply using the WiFi network in your house to transmit music.

AirPlay replaces Apple's AirTunes technology. This was an earlier music streaming system that required a couple of add-ons to work – Apple TV, and AirPort Express.

Apple TV is a device that connects to the Internet and to your television, delivering content from your PC and from the Internet to your TV. AirPort Express is a device that sets up a wireless network using your home broadband connection. You can connect it to your stereo's speakers,

allowing music to stream from your computer to the stereo.

AirPlay takes these features and adds some others – it lets you stream to the Apple TV and AirPort Express base-station directly from your iPad, iPhone, or iPod Touch. And, with AirPlay, Apple has added another twist – it has licensed the technology to a select group of third-party speaker makers (including Bowers & Wilkins and iHome) so that AirPlay compatibility can be built into speaker systems, allowing users

to wirelessly stream to their speakers straight out of the box. There's plenty of scope for more wireless streaming options in the future, as we explore over the page.

Not quite as sexy, but impressive and useful nonetheless, Apple has also added AirPrint to the iOS setup. Now, using compatible WiFi printers from HP and Epson, you can print photos, documents, web pages and more from your iPad in just a few taps.

If you're serious about using your iPad for work, then it's vital that you'll be able to print easily – and thanks to AirPrint, this is also a breeze. With the iPad's amazing media streaming capabilities, it's becoming the go-to gadget for music and more around the house. ›››

Apple TV

How the Apple TV can enhance
your home cinema experience

The Apple TV started life as a big silver box that few people really wanted. For a while, it was unclear whether even Apple knew whether there was a market for it. Now though, Apple's given it a slick, black redesign, and with the advent of AirPlay, the Apple TV has a new lease of life.

The Apple TV is an Internet-connected box that plugs into your television. Once installed, it can receive AirPlay streams from various locations – such as your computer, your iPhone, or your iPad.

To use it, you simply play music or video from your iPad's iPod or Videos app. You'll see an icon that looks like a doubled-up version of the iPad's WiFi icon. Tap that, and you'll see the option to play the media via your Apple TV. The media should stream to your television through the Apple TV – and you can use the iPad (or iPhone or iPod Touch) as a remote control from your sofa.

Future thoughts
**How AirPlay could evolve
into an industry standard**

Apple is notoriously tight with licences. But gadget companies are gradually starting to release AirPlay speakers, and rumour has it that this could be the start of a broader trend.

Business media agency Bloomberg has reported a rumour that suggests AirPlay technology could be licensed to companies that make HD televisions. This would mean you'd be able to stream movie content from your iPad 2 straight to your TV, without the need for an Apple TV.

The other rumour is that Apple are making a dedicated TV, partnering with an established TV maker and releasing a set at the end of 2012...

The AirPlay setup

Take full advantage of AirPlay on your iPad with these add-ons

Speaker systems

Apple initially licensed a handful of companies to make AirPlay-compatible speakers, and there was a huge delay in the products coming to market but there are now many available. Hi-fi experts Bowers & Wilkins, iHome, Denon, Marantz and Philips got in early and everyone from Sony to Samsung have followed. The Bowers & Wilkins Zeppelin Air was the first available in the UK and it's a beauty.

Printing unplugged

It may not sound like much, but printing from your iPad is a pretty cool feature, especially when you consider how incredibly easy it is to set up one of HP's AirPrint-compatible printers. We tested the feature using an AirPrint-compatible printer from HP. Simply plug in and switch on your printer, connect it to your local WiFi network, and hit 'Print' on the iPad's share menu. Our iPad found the printer, with no additional set-up required. Some models can even output 6 x 4in prints if you load them with glossy photo paper.

iPhone or iPod Touch

If you have an iPhone or iPod Touch, you probably have various apps and content synced to your iPad and your other iOS devices. With AirPlay, you can play all of that content on your AirPlay speaker set or on the television.

AirPort Express

If you don't want to shell out on a new iPad speaker system, you could get an AirPort Express to connect to your exising hi-fi. It costs £79 from Apple, and can also be used to connect to other USB devices, such as printers and scanners, wirelessly.

iPad Who's who

How the iPad will prove its worth whatever your job, interests or budget

Backpacker

Student

Businessperson

Teenager

Homemaker

Kid

56% 🔋

iPad ideas

Notes

Today

The iPad is useful to just about anyone – which is possibly why the whole world seems to want one right now. Thanks to some nifty hardware and the incredible App Store, the iPad really does offer something for everyone.

The accessories market, too, is teeming with gadgets and clever add-ons that will add yet more functionality to this wafer-thin slice of touchscreen genius in you hands.

So, we've put together a series of scenarios to show you just how versatile the iPad is – to give you ideas about how you and your family might be able to make use of your new gadget.

It's the ideal travel companion, study partner, and has thousands of uses around the home. It's great for work, and offers a whole new and appealing way for teaching children.

So read on to see how people – maybe people a bit like you – can get the most out of the iPad...

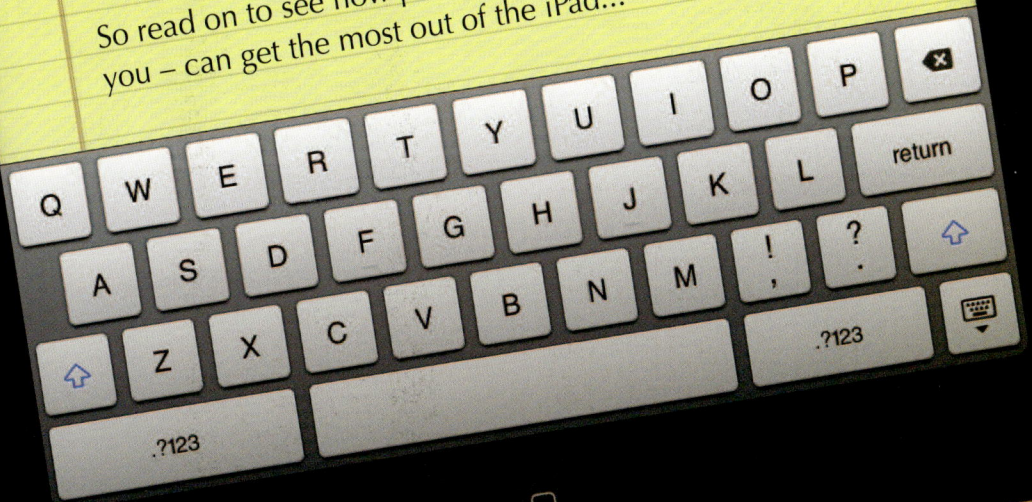

Q W E R T Y U I O P ⌫

A S D F G H J K L return

Z X C V B N M ! ? .?123

.?123 ⌨

The Businessperson

Getting down to business with the iPad

A typical day:

The Businessperson gets up early to start their day, catching up with the news on their iPad in the kitchen as they get breakfast. Their iPad can tell them about traffic incidents, train delays and Tube problems before they even set off on their journey.

During the day, the Businessperson can take notes on the iPad, use it for presentations, send emails and instant message colleagues, and even work on Office documents. And FaceTime and Skype video conferencing means there's no need to travel to another office for meetings.

Then on the commute home, the Businessperson can watch a movie or read a book – all on their iPad.

Recommended model:

New iPad WiFi + 4G (black) 16GB

4G mobile networks may not be available in the UK yet, but this model allows the Businessperson to access existing 3G networks for always-on Internet access, no matter where they are. Black spells professional and with most files on computers or the cloud, 16GB of storage should be fine.

Essential apps:
Downloads for work

Perfect accessory:

Apple VGA Adapter
£25
www.apple.com

Let's you put whatever is on your iPad on a VGA-equipped TV, monitor or external projector for video mirroring – perfect for when you want to use your iPad to make a presentation to colleagues.

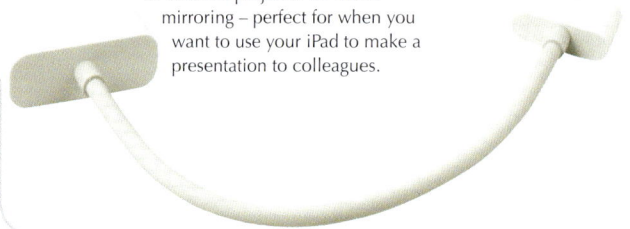

Pages
£5.99

Just like the Mac desktop equivalent, Pages for iPad is a beautifully crafted app with multiple features. It's more than just a word processor, offering page layout functions for a wide range of tasks from projects to posters.

National Rail
£4.99

For busy commuters who need to know if their train's been delayed, what time the next train is, which platform it's going from and the last train home, National Rail is indispensable.

Financial Times iPad edition
Free

Read the entire *Financial Times* specially formatted for the iPad. Customise it, watch video coverage and track stocks, and if you're going to be offline later, download all the content before you go.

The Homemaker

For chores, for entertainment and for inspiration, the iPad can't be beaten

A typical day:

The Homemaker starts the day by preparing breakfast for the family, while listening to the radio over the Internet on their iPad. After taking the kids to school, they return home to tidy the house, and do the chores, while listening to podcasts and music. The groceries that they ordered using the Tesco groceries app arrive dead on time.

If the Homemaker finally has some free time, they head off to the gym, using an iPad personal fitness training app. Then they return home to cook the evening meal using one of the many recipe apps available for the iPad.

Recommended model:

New iPad WiFi 16GB (black)

With WiFi available at almost every destination, the extra expense of 3G is unnecessary for the Homemaker. Easy access to a computer for syncing means that more storage isn't needed, so 16GB should be more than sufficient. And choosing the black edition ensures that the iPad remains spotless.

Perfect accessory:

Just Mobile Encore stand for iPad
£59.95
www.apple.com

This stylish stand securely supports your iPad in portrait and landscape mode, using rubber to avoid scratches. The adjustable fold-down arm allows you to position the iPad for optimal viewing when your hands aren't free.

Essential apps:
For the house-proud

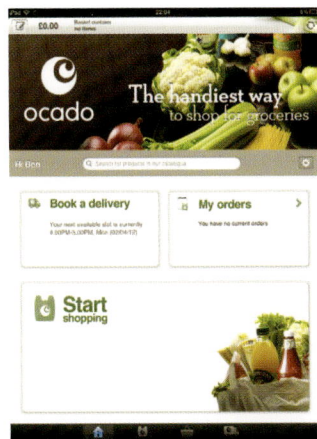

Ocado

Ocado is the famous home delivery company that carries Waitrose produce right to your door, and it was first on the scene with an app especially made for iPad.

TuneIn Radio
£0.59

Not only can you listen to radio stations from all around the world, complete with listings, including the BBC's stations, but you can also pause, rewind and record live broadcasts to play back later – vital if you're going to get interrupted a lot.

Nike Training Club
Free

Nike Training Club is a training app that provides you with your own personal trainer, anytime, anywhere. It has more than 60 custom-built workouts featuring audio guidance and on-demand instruction from a Nike Professional Trainer.

The Teenager

Stay in touch with and impress friends with the iPad

A typical day:

The Teenager wakes up and within moments is accessing Facebook on their iPad, using it to chat and find out what their friends have been up to. After leaving the house, they meet up with them, filming videos using the iPad's camera – while still keeping in touch with other friends on Facebook.

They then go to a Starbucks for coffee and use the WiFi there to look at full-screen YouTube videos or play network games.

Then, when it's time to go home, the Teenager can rent age-appropriate movies or catch up (quietly, thanks to the iPad's headphones) on TV with one of the many TV iPad apps – then say goodnight to their friends on Facebook.

Recommended model:

New iPad WiFi + 4G 32GB (white)

For always-on connectivity, the Teenager needs 3G mobile Internet access as well as WiFi, both of which are available on this model. And with all that media to watch and record, more storage is a must.

Perfect accessory:

Monitor Audio iDeck 200
£249
www.monitoraudio.co.uk

The Monitor Audio iDeck 200 is a great quality dock for iPhone and iPad which offers style, performance and loud volumes without breaking a sweat. Importantly, the sound is easily capable of filling a large room too.

Essential apps:
Keeping up to date

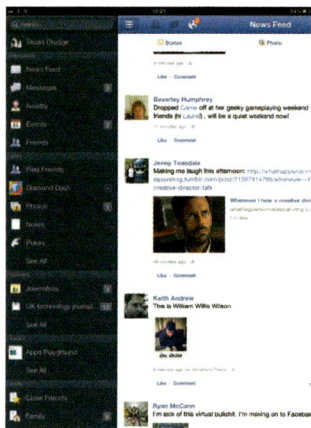

Facebook
Free

Facebook took its time creating a native app for iPad, but the result is worth it. Great for browsing your news feed and posting updates, it's particularly impressive when swiping through friends' photo albums. A very impressive social dashboard.

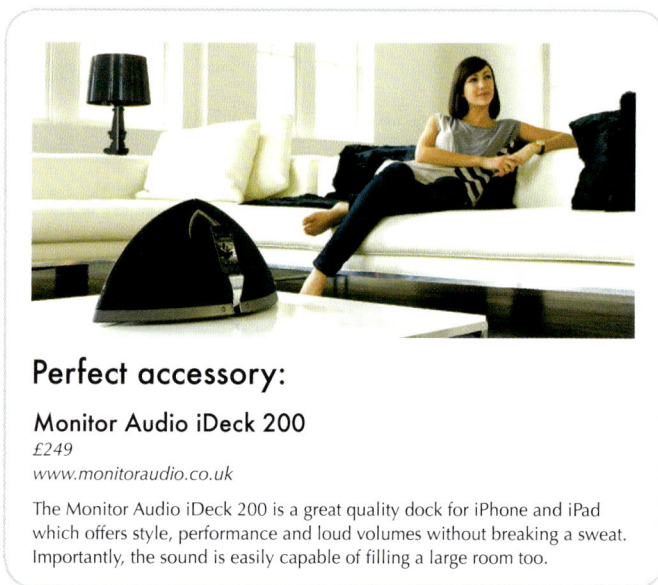

iMovie
£2.99

Make and edit movies in high definition on your iPad. Add music, photos, video and sound effects, then share them on YouTube, Facebook or Vimeo or sync them back to your Mac to do more work on them.

BBC iPlayer for iPad
Free

Watch and listen live to BBC TV and radio programmes, or catch up on your favourite BBC programmes from the last seven days. Add programmes to your favourites and have them ready and waiting when they're available.

The Kid

Keep them occupied and educated with an iPad

A typical day:

The Kid wakes up bright and early and surprises their parents while they're still in bed. So the parents give the Kid the iPad so they can watch *Finding Nemo* for the 15th time. After breakfast, the Kid can play some age-appropriate games, such as Thomas The Tank Engine, or take advantage of the iPad's camera to play the hilarious Face Melter.

To get them ahead of their classmates, the Kid can then use educational apps that teach them about spelling, numbers, music and languages, before night time comes and they can relax, once again, with *Finding Nemo*. Or an iBook.

Recommended model:

New iPad WiFi 16GB (black)

No need for bells and whistles, just the basic model for the Kid for both storage and connectivity. However, even though the iPad wipes clean, white is never a good idea with kids.

Perfect accessory:

Vogel Ringo
£69.99
www.tabletonthewall.com

Sticking your iPad on the wall essentially makes it into a TV for the kitchen or deluxe jukebox screen for AirPlay fun with your compatible AirPlay hi-fi or dock. The Vogel Ringo is sturdy and works well in the car, too. A great gadget, if a bit expensive.

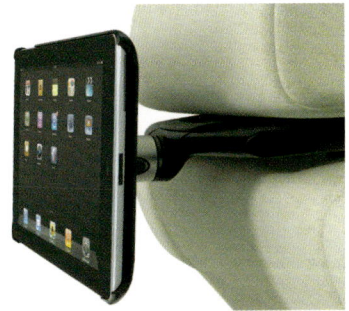

Essential apps:
For hours of fun

Draw Something
Free / £0.69

This Facebook-fuelled Pictionary-style game is the latest craze, and it's at its best on the iPad's larger screen. It's turn-based, so you needn't be online at the same time – and you can play several games at once.

Thomas & Friends: Misty Island Rescue
£2.99

Read, watch, listen and play with kids' favourite Thomas The Tank Engine and his friends. Not just a story, this includes painting, dot-to-dot, a jigsaw and other puzzles.

ABC Animals
Price £1.19

ABC Animals provides interactive flashcards that aid in teaching young children to recognise, say and print English alphabet letters. And to get them ahead, start them off in foreign languages – it includes handy French, German and Spanish flashcards.

The Student

For work, for leisure, for finding the nearest pub

A typical day:

The Student's day starts – after entering how much they drank the night before in their iPad's NHS Drinks Tracker – with lectures. Recording them for later listening or viewing with the iPad's microphone or camera, the Student can then catch up on their reading, do some research on the web, write up their work (no need for a separate laptop) or download some iTunes U lectures.

In the evening, the Student uses the iPad to look up the times of shows, movies or gigs and book tickets. Afterwards, they can use their iPad to find the nearest pub.

Recommended model:

New iPad WiFi + 4G 64GB (white)

The 4G iPad's 3G connectivity ensures that the Student has information at their fingertips or in their bag whenever they want, wherever they want. Large storage means no need for a separate laptop and their entire music collection on iTunes. And white is so non-conformist.

Perfect accessory:

Apple iPad Keyboard Dock

£56
www.apple.com

The Apple iPad Keyboard Dock gives you an actual keyboard for typing, a built in AC charger to keep the iPad's battery fully charged and a Dock for connecting and syncing to a computer (if you have one).

Essential apps:
For work and play

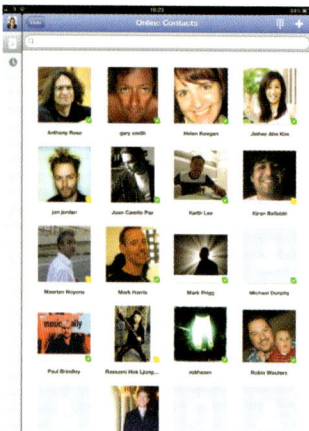

Skype for iPad
Free

Skype is one of the best Voice-over-IP apps for cheap calls to friends and family, but that's only part of its appeal. Full-screen video calls make it a viable alternative to Apple's FaceTime, especially as it can talk to non-Apple devices.

Kindle for iPad
Free

Download and read any of Amazon's 900,000+ Kindle titles, including many classic novels for free (or nearly free). You can also make notes, highlight text and search for text in books, making it essential for essays and dissertations.

Movies by Flixster
Free

Movies by Flixster lets you watch movie trailers, find screening times, search critic reviews from Rotten Tomatoes, and share movie ratings with your friends. It can find the nearest cinema, tell you what's on at what time and provide you with full booking details.

The Backpacker

The new iPad: guide, companion, souvenir-keeper

A typical day:

As soon as the Backpacker is ready for the day, they're using their iPad to look at where to go, whether it's in a guide app or on a website. They can check out times and buy tickets for trains and planes, or search for great walking routes. Then they can head off, ready to explore and take photos with their iPad.

Using a journal app, they can track their route and store notes about where they've been, before night comes when they can post their pictures and movies online, before watching the stars and learning about them with the Star Walk night sky map app.

Recommended model:

New iPad WiFi + 4G 64GB (white)

Always-on 3G and GPS are essential for the Backpacker, while the large storage means that there's plenty of room for pictures, videos and entertainment to record memories of your travels and share with friends back home. And white just looks cooler on a beach or in a café.

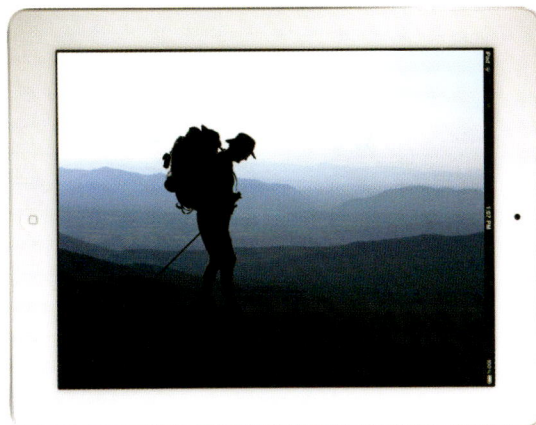

Perfect accessory:

Otterbox iPad Defender Case
£69.99
www.otterbox.com

Designed to withstand just about any environment, it has a silicone skin to absorb shocks, a polycarbonate shell and a foam interior to stop scratching. Plus the clip-on touchscreen cover has a fold-out stand – handy for FaceTiming the jealous people back home.

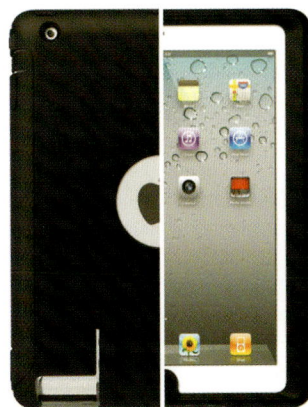

Essential apps:
Travel in style

Viewranger
Free
Get access to 10,000 trip guides using official maps for 120 countries. The UK data uses official Ordnance Survey locations which makes it ideal for GPS use as well as biking and walking trips around the country. Extra maps and features are in-app purchases.

TripAdvisor
Free

Not only can it tell you great places to go to before you head off, Trip Advisor can also tell you where to stay and eat when you're there, thanks to a wealth of user reviews. An augmented reality view will let you see where recommended places are nearby.

Twitter
Free

If you're addicted to all things Twitter, the service has a good-looking iPad app to meet all your 140 character-based needs. The interface is slick, allowing you to swipe between views such as @replies and direct messages. You can also set push notifications so you know when you receive new messages.

Start up

You've splashed your cash and got yourself a brand new iPad. What now? The tutorials over the following pages will have you up and running in no time…

At a glance – how to get started with your iPad

NEED TO KNOW
Throughout this book, you'll find these Need to Know boxes, offering vital context and explaining in more depth what you're learning to do.

EXPERT TIPS
Our tutorials are littered with expert tricks, and you'll find a wealth of insider knowledge dotted all over the Start-up and Apps in depth sections.

WANT MORE?
You may find yourself wanting to explore further. These boxes offer recommended apps and techniques for you to follow up and try out.

The basics

Your guided tour of the iPad …

Headphone jack

The iPad works with any 3.5mm headphones – the white ones that come with your iPad have a remote control for controlling music. The socket is also an input, so with the right gadgets you can use it to plug musical instruments into your iPad.

Sleep/wake

The Sleep/Wake button is located here. This lets you quickly lock the iPad when you're done using it. You also hold it down to turn the device on and off.

Hardware switch

You can define what this switch does in Settings – you can set it to lock the orientation of the screen (so that it doesn't rotate when you turn the iPad around), or you can use it as a mute switch.

Spy hole

This is the camera that allows you to take pictures of yourself in Photo Booth and have FaceTime video chats with your friends. The other camera is on the back – this lets you take pictures and shoot video, using the screen as your viewfinder.

Louder, softer

The volume switch is located here for when you're using the iPad's iPod app (and many other apps that make sound). There's also an onscreen volume slider.

Take me Home

No matter what you're doing on the iPad, the Home button will always take you back to the Home screen. Press it to exit apps. Press it again to be taken to the search screen (you can also get there by swiping left from your Home screen).

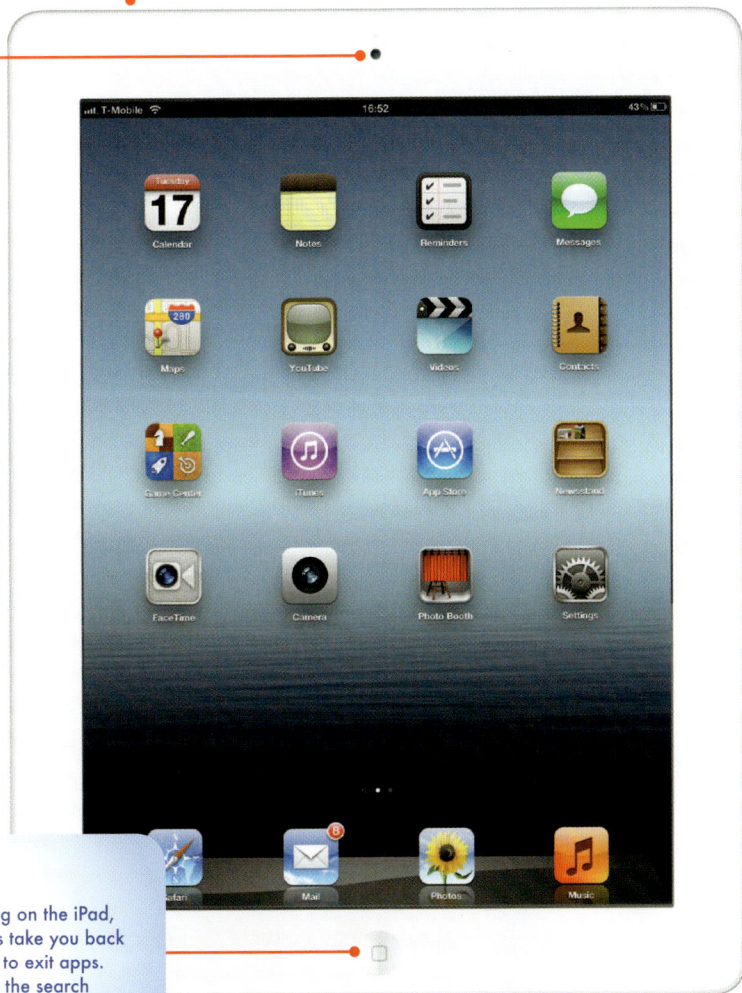

Out of the box: set up your iPad

▶ Congratulations! You've taken the plunge and bought your iPad. Remember to savour taking it out of Apple's outrageously lavish packaging, because you only get to do it once.

Now it's time to set up your iPad so you can start exploring its many features. The key to this, at least to start with, is iTunes – Apple's media management software. This started out as a music program, but now takes care of everything from apps and contacts to movies and music.

Your iPad takes its setup information from iTunes, and you 'sync' content across from your computer to your iPad, all through iTunes. So the first thing you need to do when you've taken the iPad out of its box is plug it into your computer.

Syncing content through iTunes is pretty straightforward, but there are all sorts of tricks and tweaks you can perform to get your iPad running just the way you want it to. Read on to get started.

VITAL INFO

You should only ever see this screen once – unless you later wipe your iPad and start again. Until you've plugged your iPad into your computer and started syncing content, though, this is all your iPad can do -- so that's the first step.

You will need
Your iPad
Mac with OS X 10.5.8 or later, or PC with Windows XP or later

Time required
30 minutes

Source list

This bar on the left-hand side of iTunes is called the 'Source list'. When you connect your iPad it will always appear here. Click it to edit your sync options.

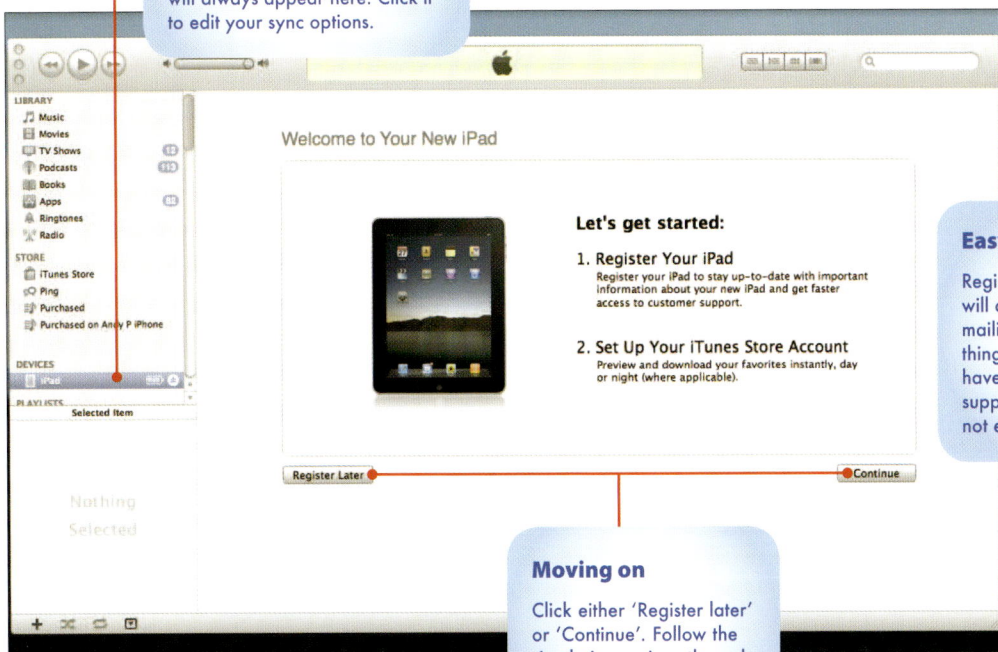

Welcome to Your New iPad

Let's get started:

1. **Register Your iPad**
   Register your iPad to stay up-to-date with important information about your new iPad and get faster access to customer support.

2. **Set Up Your iTunes Store Account**
   Preview and download your favorites instantly, day or night (where applicable).

Register Later   Continue

Easy does it

Registering your iPad will add you to the Apple mailing list and makes things easier if you need have to call customer support. However, it's not essential.

Moving on

Click either 'Register later' or 'Continue'. Follow the simple instructions through the initial setup.

NEED TO KNOW
What's an Apple ID?

An Apple ID is an online account that's linked to your credit card, so you can make quick and easy payments for apps, music, and movies. If you don't have an Apple ID you can set one up as part of your iPad setup.

Apple ID

If you have an Apple ID, sign in below. Otherwise choose "I do not have an Apple ID," choose your country, and click Continue.

You may already have an Apple ID if you have made purchases from the iTunes Store, Apple Store, or have previously registered an iPhone.

○ Use my Apple ID to register my iPad

Apple ID
[and]
Example: steve@mac.com

Password

Forgot Password?

○ I do not have an Apple ID

I live in: [United Kingdom ▾]

Cancel   Continue

...ts reserved. | Privacy Policy | Terms of Service | Terms of Sale

Apple ID

If you have an Apple ID you can use it to register your iPad using those details. If you don't have one, set one up by ticking this bottom circle to indicate that you need one.

Step-by-step guide ❯❯❯

Getting set up

Using iTunes, you can add content such as music, books and films and even your address book to your iPad. iTunes is also where apps – and other content you've downloaded to your iPad – back up to when you connect the device to your computer. Here's how to get started.

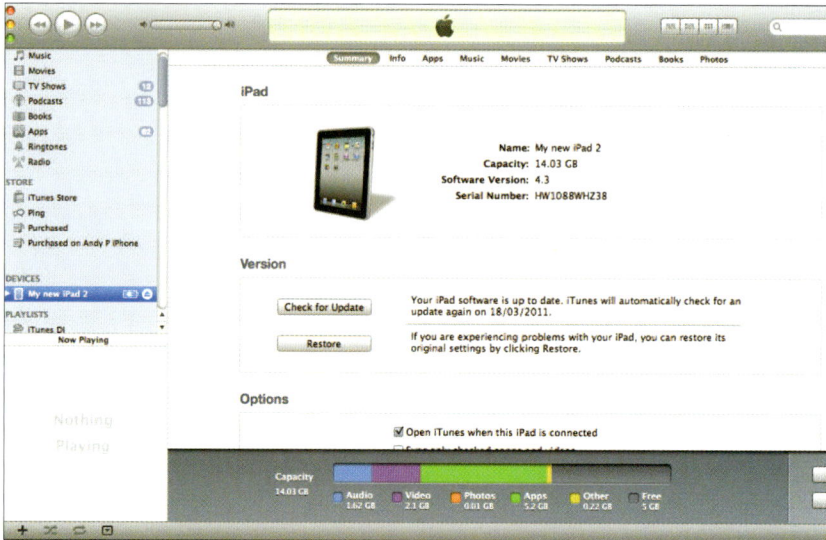

EXPERT TIP
Hopefully you'll never need it, but if you have problems with your iPad you can hit 'Restore' here. Your iPad should automatically back up each time you plug it in, so you will only lose data added since your last backup.

1 The summary screen shows you information about your iPad at a glance. The bar at the bottom shows how much space on the iPad's flash memory you have left. Then there's a button to check for software updates, and options controlling how iTunes responds when you connect the iPad to your computer.

2 The Info tab lets you sync information such as contacts or the Calendar, from your computer to your iPad's built-in apps. You can also sync email accounts. To do this you will need your email set up in the Mail app on your Mac, or Outlook Express, Outlook 2003 or later, Windows Contacts, or the Windows Address Book.

3 This is where things get interesting: in the Music tab, you can sync your music to your iPad. This takes music from your iTunes library and copies it to the iPod app on your iPad. This means you can listen to tunes on the move, and also enables certain apps to use your music – including several that help you learn to play instruments.

Summary | Info | Apps | Music | Movies | TV Shows | Podcasts | Books | Photos

☑ Sync Apps   My new iPad   114 apps

Sort by Kind

iPhone and iPod touch Apps

☑ Travel		2.4 MB
☑ **Daytrotter** Music		1.4 MB
☑ **Dishy – Cooking Made Ea...** Lifestyle		6.5 MB
☑ **EasyBeats Pro Drum Mach...** Music		16.2 MB
☑ **Facebook** Social Networking		6.5 MB
☑ **Fidelio** Utilities		5.3 MB
☑ **FIFA 11 by EA SPORTS™** Games		1.05 GB
☑ **FindaProperty.com Search...** Lifestyle		9.7 MB
☑ **FlipBook Lite** Entertainment		1.1 MB
☑ **FourTrack** Music		6.5 MB
☑ **Fuel Calculator Lite** Utilities		420 KB
☑ **Goldfrapp Pinball**		

4 The Apps tab is where iTunes backs up all the apps you've downloaded to your device. This means if something goes wrong with your iPad, your apps collection isn't lost. You can drag and drop apps from the list on the left onto the picture of your iPad, and even rearrange them on your iPad's home screen through this iTunes screen.

5 Movies, TV shows, podcasts and books – both audiobooks and ebooks – sync in much the same way. iTunes stores and organises content, ready for syncing to a mobile device such as the iPad. Scroll through the tabs at the top to set your syncing preferences, keeping an eye on how much free space you have in the bottom bar.

6 You can also add photos to your iPad using iTunes. On a Mac you can set the iPad to sync photos and photo albums from iPhoto, or you can pick a folder on your Mac or PC for iTunes to sync to your iPad. When you've chosen all the content you want to transfer, click 'Apply' in the bottom-right corner and wait for the content to copy.

EXPERT TIP

In the Summary screen, you can set your iPad to convert high bit rate tracks down to 128kbps. This will save space on your iPad if you're syncing a lot of high-quality music.

Get to know the iOS 5.1 interface

▶ You will navigate around your iPad's apps and content using Apple's slick iOS interface. The iOS has come a long way since it was introduced on the first iPhone – and even that was pretty impressive when it emerged in 2007. Now in version 5.1, iOS incorporates many new tweaks and technologies that make using your iPad easier and more fun than before. You can now take advantage of new camera functions on the new iPad, delete photos from your online Photo Stream and enjoy better movie controls when viewing your rentals from the iTunes Store...

VITAL INFO

This tutorial will show you how to multitask and manage running apps, and how to organise your apps into folders.

What you need
Your iPad

Time required
10 minutes

Swipe for apps

Once you've got more than just the default apps on your iPad, they'll appear over multiple home pages. Swipe left and right to view them.

Page turner

These dots show how many pages of apps you have and what page you're on. They're always visible from the home page.

Search party

Swipe left from your first page of apps to the little magnifying glass on the page indicator to search your iPad.

Quick Wiki

At the bottom of your search results, you'll find quick links to search Wikipedia or Safari for the search terms you have entered.

Dictation

Available on the new iPad. Simply press the mic button and let your iPad write your words on screen. Requires a WiFi connection at all times.

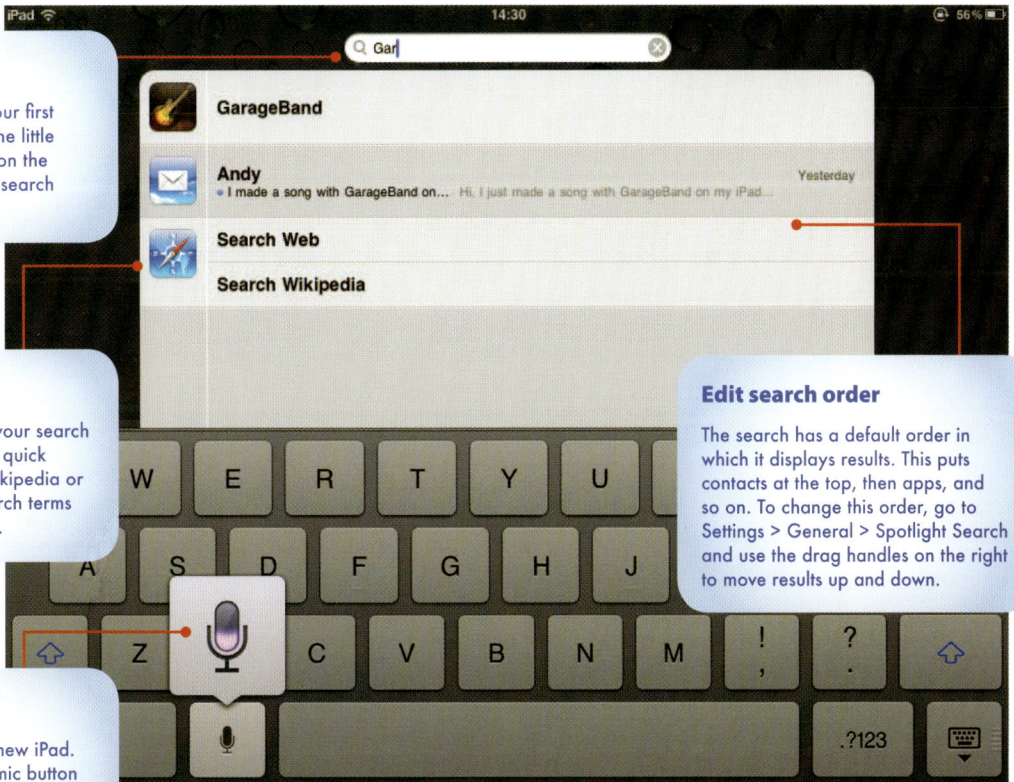

Edit search order

The search has a default order in which it displays results. This puts contacts at the top, then apps, and so on. To change this order, go to Settings > General > Spotlight Search and use the drag handles on the right to move results up and down.

Step-by-step guide ⟫⟫

1 You know by now what the iPad home screen looks like. Apple's built-in apps and all the others you download appear here. But if Apple's default icon arrangement doesn't suit you, it's time to customise.

2 Tap and hold any app icon until the icons start to wobble. Now you can drag them around. You can even edit the bottom row of icons, which appear on every page. Tap the 'Home' button to set your layout.

3 Folders offer another way to manage your apps. To create one, just tap and hold an app so that they wobble, then drag one icon onto another. The iPad will create a folder with both apps inside.

WANT MORE? *Rename Folders*

The iPad will automatically name your folder based on the apps you put in it – but you can edit this. When you create a folder, tap the automatic name and the keyboard will spring up for you to enter your own.

4 When you open apps they stay open, even if you navigate away from them. Double-tap the 'Home' button to see a list of all the apps that are open in a 'tray' at the bottom of the screen. This can run to several pages.

5 Running a lot of apps simultaneously can affect battery life. To close apps you no longer need to have open, go to your apps tray, then tap and hold one. The icons will wobble, and you can tap the '-' sign to close individual apps.

NEED TO KNOW
Quick access

By default, the bottom row of apps has four icons on it, but you can drag up to six apps (and even folders) onto it. These are visible on every page for easy access.

6 You can also organise your apps using iTunes on your computer. Connect your iPad to your computer, and in iTunes select Apps in the top bar. You'll see a visual representation of your home screens and you can drag and drop apps. Even apps you've deleted from your iPad are stored here, if you backed them up.

NEED TO KNOW
iPod controls

If you have music playing while you're do other things on your iPad, there's a quick way to control it. Double-tap the 'Home' button and swipe to the left. You'll see controls for your music, as well as a button to edit screen brightness.

Buy apps, music and more from the iTunes Store

▶ The iTunes Store is the essential element in your iPad's setup that turns a good user experience into a great one. iTunes started as a humble media manager; now it hosts an online store selling music, movies, TV shows, books, and the all-important apps.

With over half a million apps and 20 million music tracks available, it's no wonder iTunes has proved so popular. More than 225 million user accounts have so far been registered, and Apple recently celebrated the download of its 25 billionth app.

Over the next few pages, you'll learn how to buy and download content directly using your iPad. You can also access the iTunes Store and App Store using iTunes on your desktop – indeed, you may already have used the iTunes Store for music. If you have, you'll use the same account details when you shop using your iPad.

If you haven't yet got an iTunes account, it's easy to set one up. All you need is your iPad (or your computer) and a credit or debit card.

VITAL INFO

This tutorial walks you through getting an iTunes account, and shopping on the iTunes and App Stores.

What you need
Your iPad
WiFi connection
An iTunes account and Apple ID
A credit card

Time required
1 hour

Shop now, pay later

Apple makes it easy to set up an iTunes account. You can browse the stores, and set up your payment account when you've found something you want to buy.

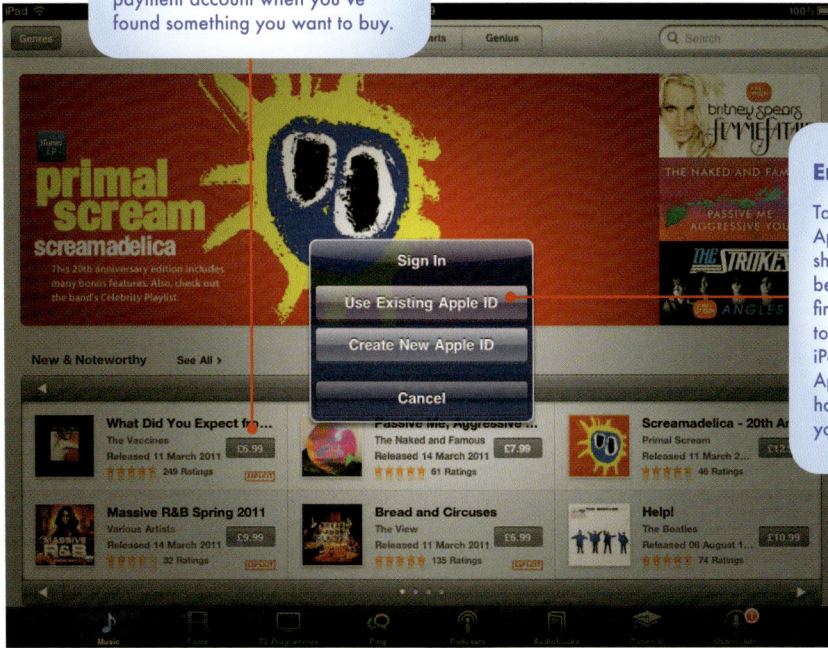

Enter password

Tap 'Use existing Apple ID' if you've shopped on iTunes before. When you first sync your device to your computer, the iPad will import your Apple ID, so all you'll have to do is enter your password.

Or try...

You can also set up or log into your iTunes account through the iPad's Settings app. Hit 'Store' on the left-hand panel, then tap 'Sign in'.

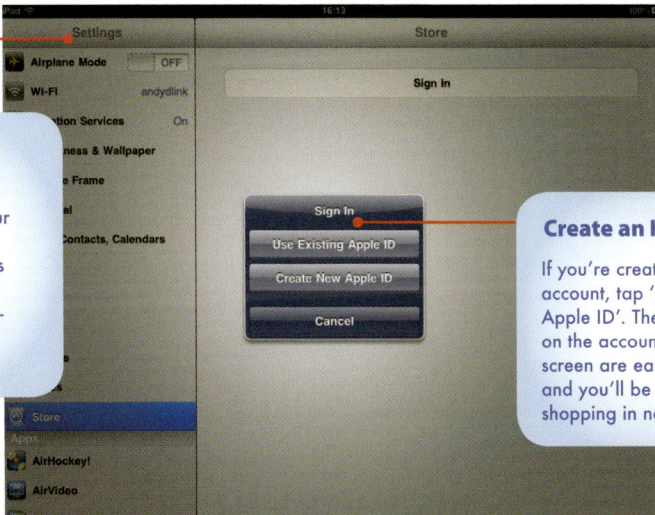

Create an ID

If you're creating a new account, tap 'Create New Apple ID'. The instructions on the account-creation screen are easy to follow, and you'll be set up for shopping in no time.

App-solutely fabulous

Time to boost your iPad's capabilities and transform it into the ultimately customised device by choosing from the massive range of apps available from the App Store.

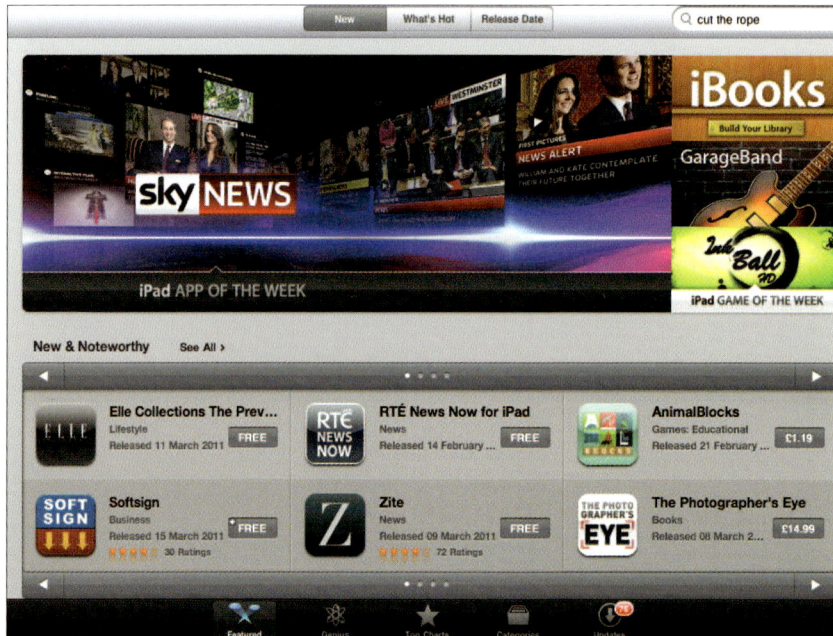

1 Launch the App Store from the home screen of your iPad and you'll be taken to the store's front page. Click the 'New' and 'What's Hot' tabs at the top of the screen to see featured apps. 'Release Date' shows you the very newest apps on the market.

2 If you're looking to find a specific app (perhaps one you've read about in the feature on page 82), tap the Search bar and type in the name. You can also enter keywords if you're looking for an app for a specific task – for example, you could search for 'Google Calendar' and see what the App Store offers.

3 Tap an app on the Store to be taken to its page. Here you'll find a summary of the app's features, see screenshots, and read what other users have to say about it. If you want to buy it, tap the price of the app. The button will turn green and read 'Buy app' (or 'Install app' if it's free). Tap again to take the plunge.

read about in the feature on page 82

EXPERT TIP

App developers are always updating their software. Once you've downloaded an app, future updates are free. The Store alerts you to updates with a badge on the 'Updates' button, in the bottom-right of the store screen. It also puts a badge on the Store icon on your home screen.

4 Now it comes to payment. If you've followed the instructions on page 29, you should already have an account, so you'll simply need to enter your password to authorise the purchase. It's worth noting that even if an app is listed as free, you'll still need an Apple ID to download it.

5 The App Store will close, and you'll be taken to your home screen. The icon of the app you've just paid for will appear on your home screen, with a progress bar that indicates how much of the app has been downloaded so far. When the progress bar disappears, the app is installed and ready to use.

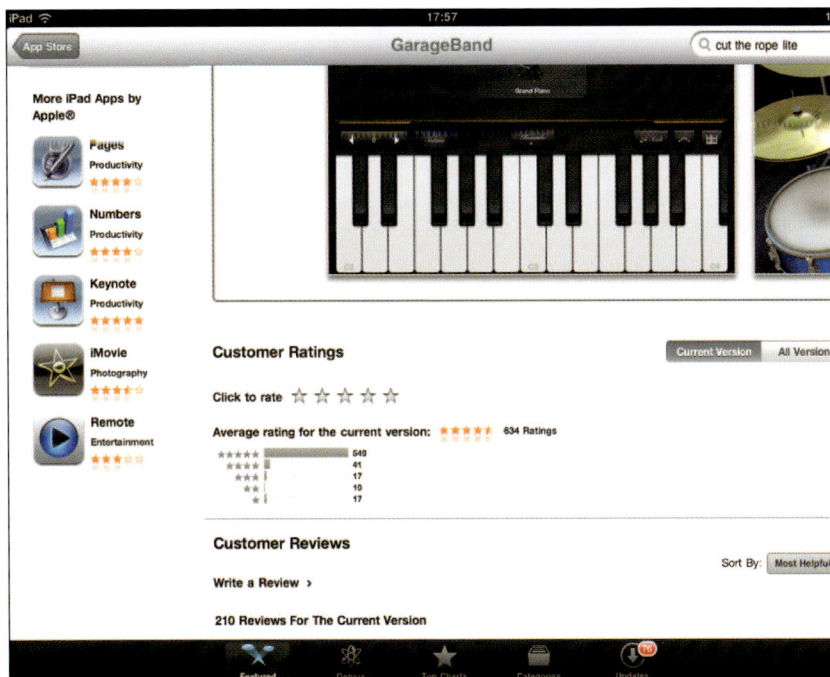

WANT MORE?
Make music
In this tutorial we're buying and downloading GarageBand onto the iPad. It's not just for show – head to page 108 for the lowdown on how to use this amazing piece of software.

6 The App Store allows you to write reviews of apps you've downloaded, or simply contribute star ratings, to help other users make up their minds. Once you've got to know an app, simply navigate to the app's page on the Store, scroll down to the reviews, and tap 'Write a Review' at the top of the list.

Get playing on the iTunes Store

The iPad is great for productivity, but it really comes into its own as an entertainment device – thanks to the colossal range of music, films and more on the iTunes Store.

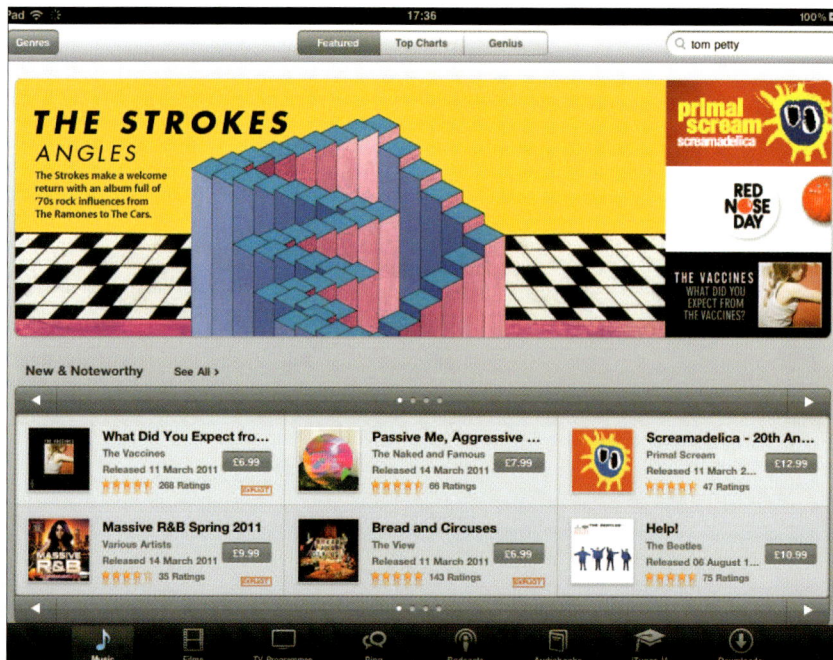

1 The iTunes Store works in a similar way to the App Store, and now offers loads of different kinds of content. The home page displays new and noteworthy recordings, and if you scroll down you'll find things like the free single of the week and forthcoming albums to pre-order.

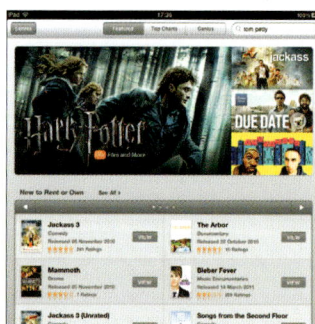

2 The buttons at the bottom of the screen take you to other areas of the store, where you can browse movies, TV programmes, podcasts, audiobooks, and iTunes U content to download. Tap a section of the Store and have a look around – or use the Search tool to look for something specific.

3 We've found the Tom Petty classic *Free Fallin'* for the bargain price of 59p, so we're going to snap that up. Tap the price, then tap the 'Buy now' button that appears. Enter your password and the song will download. Tap the 'Downloads' button at the bottom-right of the screen to track the progress.

EXPERT TIP

Keep an eye out on the iTunes Store for bargains. Apple offers a range of films to rent each week for just 99p. There's also a free single of the week, usually from an up-and-coming artist.

4 Once the download is finished, tap 'Purchased' in the top-right (or simply open the iPod app). The downloaded music will appear in your iPod interface with all the music synced from your computer. It's now all yours to play and listen to on your iPad. But the file isn't locked inside your iPad forever…

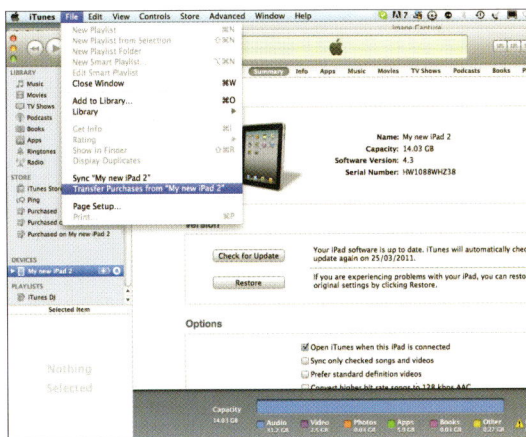

5 You can transfer the music you've purchased to your computer when you next connect the two together. Then, if you ever lose your iPad, your music is backed up on iTunes on your computer. It also means you can copy it to other devices. In iTunes, go to File > Transfer Purchases.

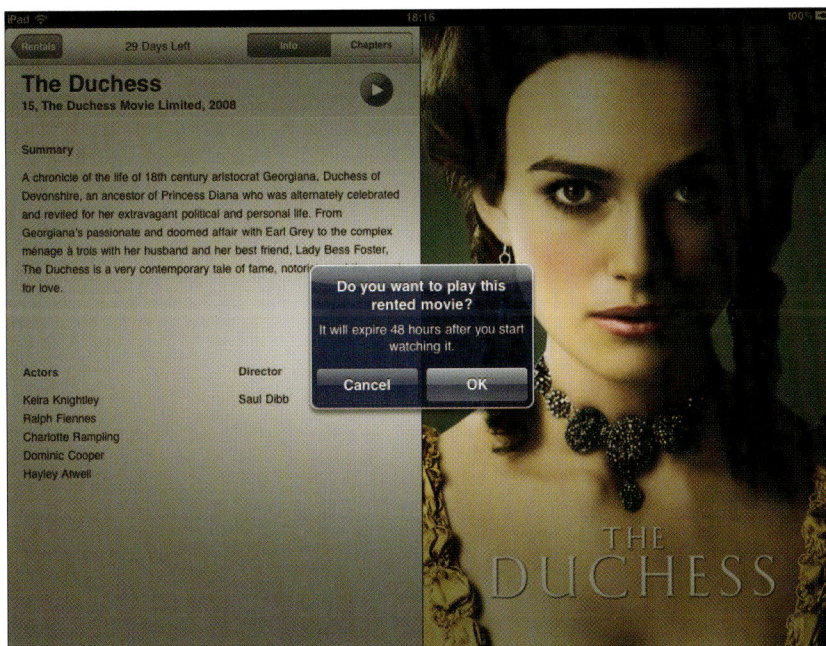

WANT MORE?
Try out Ping

Check out Ping – Apple's music and media-focused social network. Ping lets you share what you've downloaded with the world, so that everyone can see what great taste you have. Tap 'Ping' at the bottom of the Store home page to investigate.

6 Movie rentals work in a slightly different way. Once the movie is downloaded onto your iPad, you can transfer it to your computer and then to any iOS device. Once you download a rental, you have 30 days to start watching it. Once you start watching it, you have 24 hours to finish it before the rental expires.

Buy and read books with the iBooks app

▶ When the iPad launched, many people were excited at the prospect of reading books on the device, and ebooks have caught on quickly. Apple's iBookstore has been a huge hit, with nearly 200 million downloads since it opened in 2010, while Amazon's e-reader gadget, the Kindle, was among that company's best-selling products of the 2011 Christmas shopping season.

The iBooks app incorporates both the iBookstore for buying and downloading books, and the interface, for actually reading books on your iPad. The iBookstore interface is familiar if you've used the iTunes Store and App Store that we've explored on the previous pages. Its virtual bookshelves stock everything from new bestsellers to reference books, and you'll often find classics for free or for a nominal fee. The reading element of the app is highly intuitive, so read on to get started.

VITAL INFO

We'll show you how to download books from the iBookstore and read them in the iBooks app.

What you need
Your iPad
WiFi connection
An iTunes account and Apple ID
A credit card

Time required
1 hour

Tap to control

If you can't see these controls on your screen, just tap anywhere on the page once to bring them up.

Contents

This button takes you to your book's contents page. In contents you can see the chapter points in the book, and any bookmarks you add.

not to let the bees know you're coming. Now, if you have a green balloon, they might think you were only part of the tree, and not notice you, and if you have a blue balloon, they might think you were only part of the sky, and not notice you, and the question is: Which is most likely?'

'Wouldn't they notice *you* underneath the balloon?' you asked.

'They might or they might not,' said Winnie-the-Pooh. 'You never can tell with bees.' He thought for a moment and said: 'I shall try to look like a small black cloud. That will deceive them.'

'Then you had better have the blue balloon,' you said; and so it was decided.

Well, you both went out with the blue balloon, and you took your gun with you, just in case, as you always did, and Winnie-the-Pooh went to a very muddy place

that he knew of, a til he was black all over; and the blown up as big as were both holding go suddenly, and fully up into the level with the top of the tree and about twenty feet away from it.

'Hooray!' you shouted.

'Isn't that fine?' shouted Winnie-the-Pooh down to you. 'What do I look l

'You look like a bear holding on to loon,' you said.

'Not,' said Pooh anxiously, '—no small black cloud in a blue sky?'

'Not very much.'

'Ah, well, perhaps from up here it looks different. And, as I say, you never can tell

Fonts

Choose one of six fonts for your reading. You can also change the font size by hitting the small and large 'A' buttons.

A   A

Fonts

Sepia   OFF

III

It was almost two when they went into the dining-room. Back and forth over the deserted tables a heavy pattern of beams and shadows swayed with the motion of the pines outside. Two waiters, piling plates and talking loud Italian, fell silent when they came in and brought them a tired version of the table d'hôte luncheon.

"I fell in love on the beach," said Rosemary.

"Who with?"

"First with a whole lot of people who looked nice. Then with one man."

"Did you talk to him?"

"Just a little. Very handsome. With reddish hair." She was eating ravenously. "He's married though — it's usually the way."

Her mother was her best friend and had put every last possibility into the guiding of her, not so rare a thing in the theatrical profession, but rather special in that Mrs. Elsie Speers was not recompensing herself for a defeat of her own. She had no personal bitterness or resentments about life — twice satisfactorily married and twice widowed, her cheerful stoicism had each time deepened. One of her husbands had been a cavalry officer and one an army doctor, and they both left something to her that she tried to present intact to Rosemary. By not sparing Rosemary she had made her hard — by not sparing her own labor and devotion she had cultivated an idealism in Rosemary, which at present was directed toward herself and saw the world through her eyes. So that while Rosemary was a "simple" child she was protected by a double

Set bookmarks

Tap the little bookmark icon to drop a red tab over the page. This sets a bookmark, which will appear in the table of contents so you don't lose your page.

Brightness

Alter the brightness of your screen with this slider – great for reading under different lighting conditions.

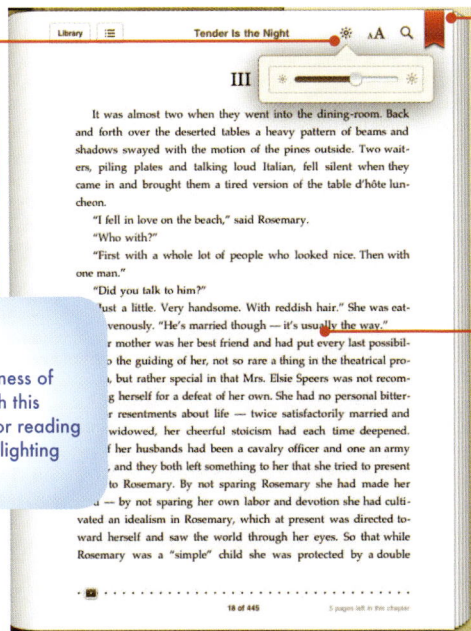

Orientation

If you hold your iPad in landscape orientation, you'll get the spread view, as above. Or, rotate it into portrait orientation to focus on one page at a time.

NEED TO KNOW
Page turner

To turn the page while reading, you can either swipe left and right across the screen, or just tap the left or right sides of the page to go back and forth.

Step-by-step guide ▶▶▶

1 iBooks gives you access to Apple's popular virtual bookshop, iBookstore, which has seen more than 700,000,000 titles downloaded so far, many of them for free. The iBooks app isn't installed by default on your new iPad, though, so you have to download it from the App Store. Don't worry, it's free!

2 Once you've downloaded iBooks, open it. The app will ask if you want to sync bookmarks across multiple devices – useful if you're reading the same book on multiple devices (such as an iPhone or iPod Touch). You'll then see your empty virtual bookshelf, so tap 'Store' in the top left corner to get started.

3 The iBookstore interface will be familiar if you've already played with the iTunes Store or App Store. Use the buttons along the bottom of the screen to browse. The first two give you a shop-style browsing experience, whereas the 'Browse' button offers you a more detailed search tool.

EXPERT TIP

Apple offers iPad, iPhone, and iPod Touch user guides on the iBookstore. They are free, and well worth keeping in your Library as a reference aid.

4 When you've found a book you'd like to read, you can tap its cover to read a synopsis, see related titles, and read customer reviews. You can also download a sample. Once you've decided, tap the price and then 'Buy book'. The book will download, and your view will flip back to your Library.

5 Back in the Library, you can watch your download's progress. When it's finished, you're ready to open up your book and read it. Tap the cover of the book you want to read, and get your view set up with the right font size and typeface, using the button in the top-right of the screen.

WANT MORE?
Kindle app

If you've got a Kindle, there is a Kindle app for iPad and iPhone which allows you to sync your bookmarks between the iOS device and the Kindle. Search the App Store for 'Kindle' to download it for free.

6 iBooks reads various document formats, including PDFs. When you receive an email attachment in a compatible format, you can save and view the file in your iBooks Library. To remove a document or book from your library, tap the 'Edit' button on the library screen.

Setting up Mail accounts on your iPad

▶ Whatever your occupation, accessing your email on the go is essential these days. But on a smartphone, this can be a cramped and awkward experience. Luckily your iPad is absolutely perfect for it.

It's incredibly easy to set up an iPad to send and receive your email. You can set up multiple accounts and arrange for all messages to arrive in one inbox, and you can do just about everything you'd want to do on a desktop email client – all from the comfort of your iPad.

So fire up the Mail app on your iPad and follow these simple instructions to get your email accounts connected.

VITAL INFO

Get up and running with an email account on your iPad, and learn how to use the Mail app.

What you need
Your iPad
An email account

Time required
20 minutes

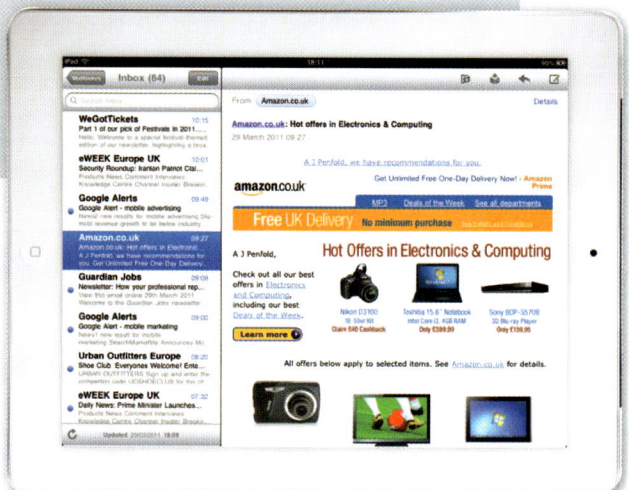

Set up your email in three steps

1 Open the Mail app from the home screen. This brings up the options for connecting to an email account. We're going to set up a Google Mail account. If you have a different email account the iPad can handle that too.

2 Enter your username and password. The process is pretty similar whether you're setting up a Google Mail, Microsoft Exchange, Yahoo! or whatever other email account you have. Just add your details and the app will verify your password.

3 Once your details are verified, you'll be asked if you want to also import notes and your calendar from your Google account. Once you've made your choices, tap 'Save'. Your mail will download and you're ready to go.

How to set up POP or IMAP Mail accounts

Although the iPad provides you with options to set up accounts for popular mail services, that's no good if you already have your own email hosted elsewhere. Here's how to set up an email account using the mysterious 'Other' option…

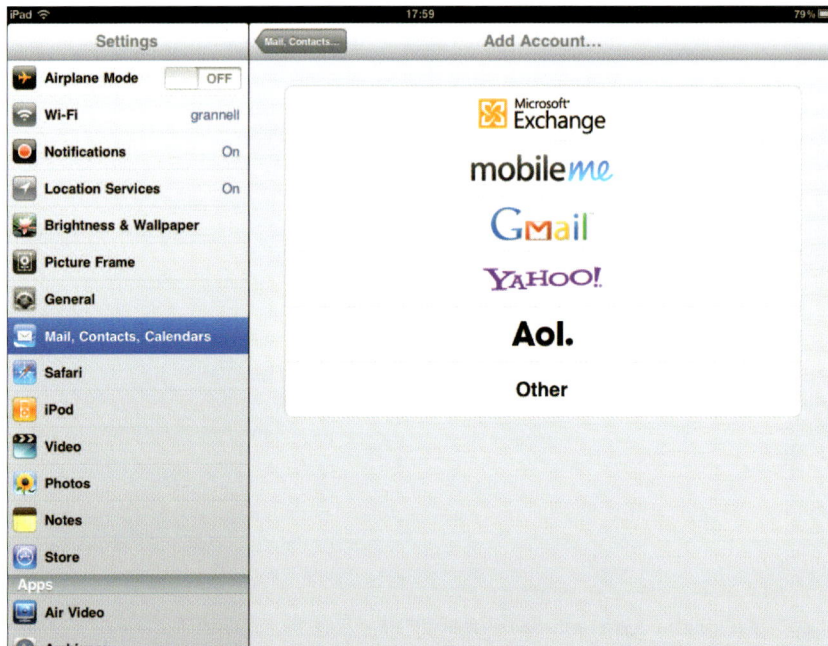

1 Launch the Settings app and select 'Mail, Contacts, Calendars' from the sidebar. Under Accounts, tap 'Add Account…' and you'll see the familiar screen with a number of email options. Tap 'Other' and on the following screen, tap 'Add Mail Account'.

2 In the 'New Account' dialog that pops up, add the email account's sender name (Name), the email address itself (Address), the password provided to you by your email host to access the POP/IMAP service (Password), together with a short description of the account.

3 Tap 'Next' and select whether you're setting up an IMAP or POP account by tapping the relevant tab (if unsure, talk to your email host/system administrator). Add details regarding your account's incoming and outgoing mail servers to the relevant fields.

NEED TO KNOW
POP vs IMAP

Most email accounts are either Post Office Protocol (POP), a download-and-delete-style service, or Internet Message Access Protocol (IMAP), which keeps all your email in sync with a remote server.

4 Tap 'Save' and your account details will be verified. In event of an error, the dialog shown above will appear. Should that happen, check and re-enter your details and tap 'Save' again. When successful, you'll be returned to 'Mail, Contacts, Calendars'.

5 Tap an account in 'Mail, Contacts, Calendars' to view additional settings. Here, you can temporarily disable the account, amend server information, or scroll down, tap Advanced and define options for message deletion and authentication.

6 Within the initial settings page of an account, there's also a large and red 'Delete Account' button. Tap that and you'll see a confirmation dialog. Tap 'Delete' and the email account and its associated messages will be removed from your iPad.

WANT MORE?
Mail Sync

If you use Mail on the Mac or Outlook on Windows, don't bother setting up email on your iPad – instead, connect your device to iTunes, access the 'Info' section, check 'Sync Mail Accounts' and sync.

Personalise Mail

Your iPad offers countless customisation options, and the Mail app gives you ample opportunities to tweak settings so it's just right for how you want to use it. From font sizes to signatures, here's how to set put your own stamp on Mail.

Customise email

Go to the Settings app and tap 'Mail, Contacts, Calendars'. It will lead you to this screen, giving you loads of options for setting up your mail.

Tweak the preview

These options let you customise how your lists of emails appear. Select the number of recent messages in the list, the length of the preview, and your font size.

Organise by thread

Viewing message threads means that all messages in a single conversation are placed in a single thread. It makes it easy to see conversations, but you can turn it off to view a list of individual messages if you prefer

Copy me in

You can set to always copy yourself into messages you write. This can help you keep track of messages sent from your iPad when you return to your desktop.

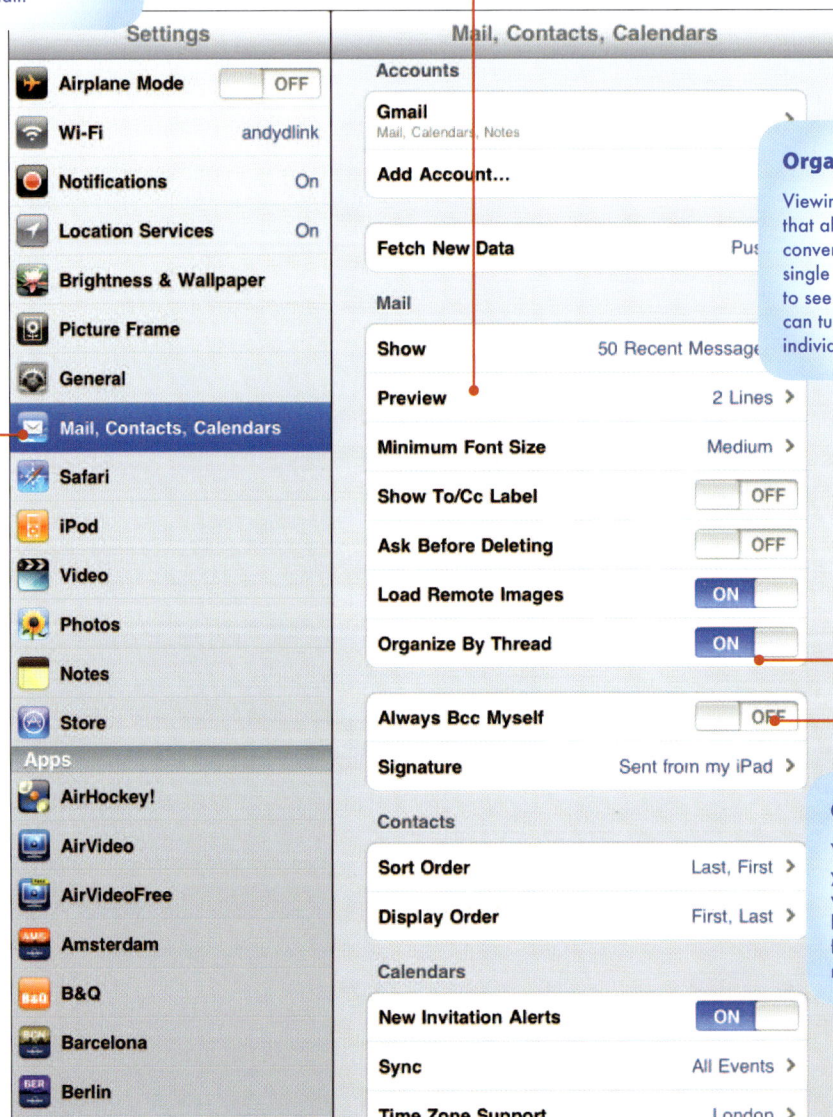

Settings

Airplane Mode		OFF
Wi-Fi		andydlink
Notifications		On
Location Services		On
Brightness & Wallpaper		
Picture Frame		
General		
Mail, Contacts, Calendars		
Safari		
iPod		
Video		
Photos		
Notes		
Store		

Apps

AirHockey!
AirVideo
AirVideoFree
Amsterdam
B&Q
Barcelona
Berlin

Mail, Contacts, Calendars

Accounts

Gmail
Mail, Calendars, Notes

Add Account...

Fetch New Data   Pus

Mail

Show	50 Recent Message
Preview	2 Lines >
Minimum Font Size	Medium >
Show To/Cc Label	OFF
Ask Before Deleting	OFF
Load Remote Images	ON
Organize By Thread	ON
Always Bcc Myself	OFF
Signature	Sent from my iPad >

Contacts

Sort Order	Last, First >
Display Order	First, Last >

Calendars

New Invitation Alerts	ON
Sync	All Events >
Time Zone Support	London >

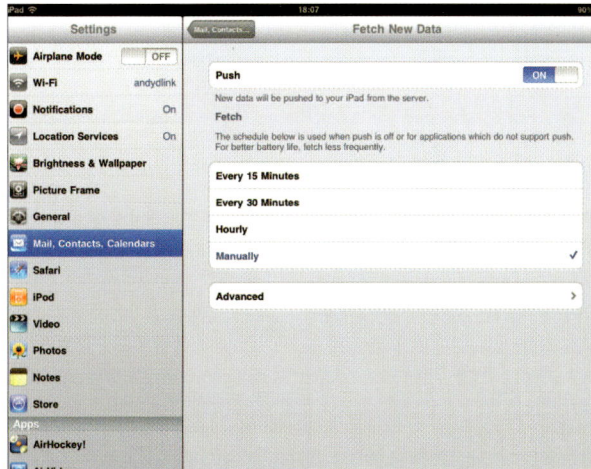

1 Your iPad can check for messages at regular intervals, or you can set it to 'Push' messages from the server, meaning you will be alerted of new emails as soon as they arrive.

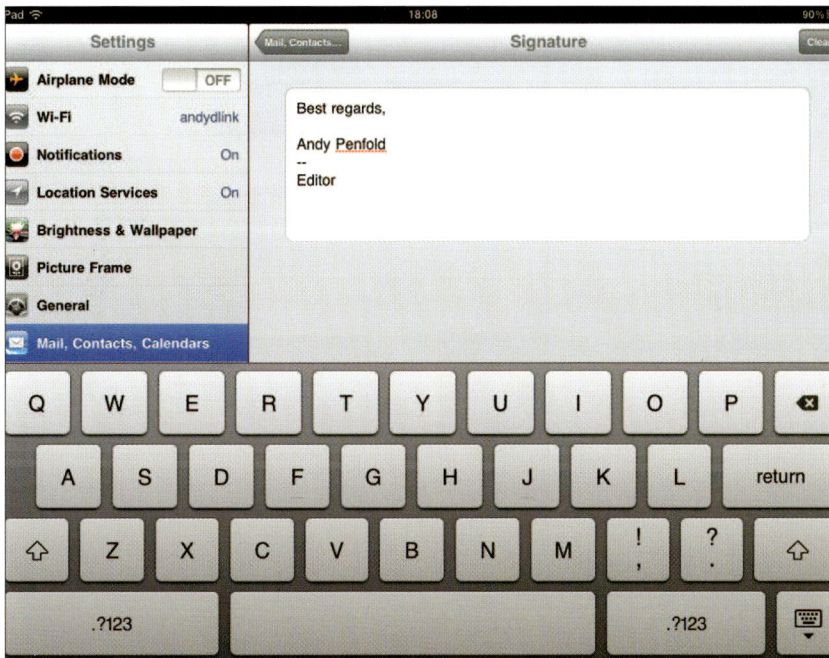

2 The default signature reads 'Sent from my iPad', which is fine for telling your mates you've just bought one, but a bit smug the rest of the time. Personalise email sign-off in 'Signature'.

Mail: a guided tour

Now you're all set up to use Mail, here's a guided tour of the app. You'll be running your digital communications from your iPad in no time, thanks to Mail's easy interface and the iPad's portability.

1 Fire up Mail and you'll find the account you've set up. In portrait mode, you get a full-screen view of your emails. Tap 'Inbox' at the top left to see a pop-up window of your message list.

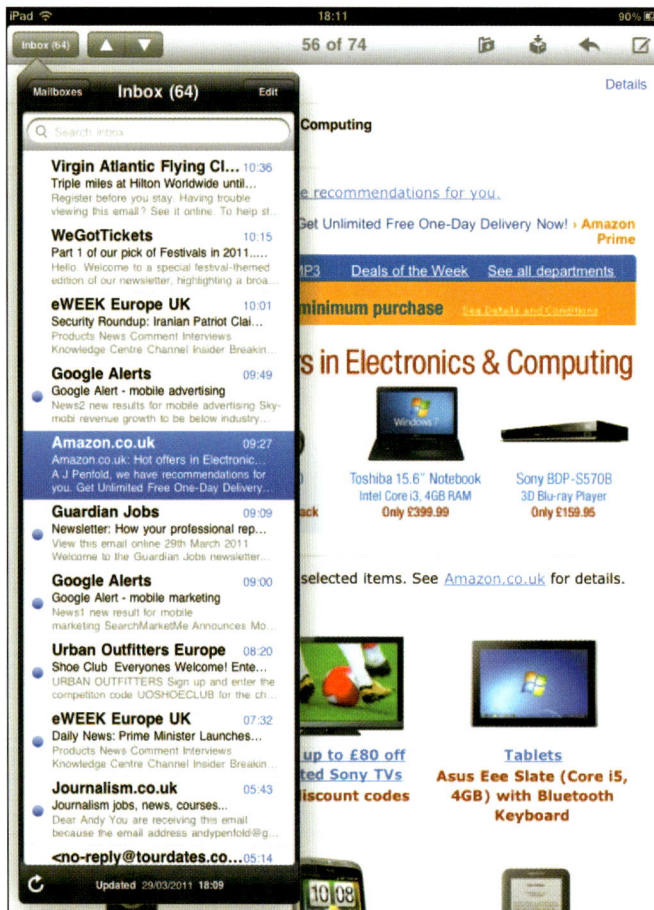

2 Turn your iPad to landscape mode and you get a split-screen view, with your inbox on the left and the full selected message on the right. To remove emails from your Inbox list, tap 'Edit'.

3 This allows you to 'Archive' messages, so that they no longer appear in your Inbox but will be kept on your Gmail server. Tap the circle next to unwanted messages so that the circle fills with a red tick icon, then press 'Archive'.

WANT MORE?
Delete vs Archive

If you want to use your iPad to permanently delete email from your Google account, go to Settings > Mail, Contacts, Calendars and tap your Gmail account. You can turn Archiving off on the next screen – this turns Mail's 'Archive' button into a 'Delete' button.

4 Time to get emailing. Press the curved arrow in the top right to reply to a message, or the pen-and-paper icon in the corner to write a new email. If you've synced contacts from your computer, press the '+' sign in the 'To' field to choose a contact.

5 If you've received a message from someone new, select the message and tap that person's name at the top of the message. You can then easily create a contact in your Contacts app straight from Mail.

6 Depending on their file size, attachments do not always download automatically. If an incoming email has files attached, you may need to tap them to start the downloading process.

EXPERT TIP

Download the iBooks app from the App Store (it's free), and you can open many attachments from Mail in that app. You can also save attached photos into the Photos app – just tap and hold the picture in Mail.

Get organised with the iPad's Calendar app

▶ Thanks to its built-in productivity apps, the iPad is a fantastic organisational device. Mail keeps you connected, while Calendar keeps you organised. The iPad's Calendar app can be synced with Outlook on a PC and Mail on the Mac, as well as offering limited support for online calendars such as Google Calendar. It also works brilliantly as a standalone organiser.

The interface is designed like a real-world diary, but it's far more useful than your bog standard paper diary. Calendar can remind you with audio and visual alarms when an appointment is coming up, and it's easy to manage events using its many onscreen tools. Here's how to set up and use Calendar on your iPad.

VITAL INFO

If you so desire (and you nearly always have your iPad with you), the Calendar app can be used as your main diary. Otherwise, you just need your PC or Mac and your iPad.

What you need
Your iPad
Some appointments

Time required
15 minutes

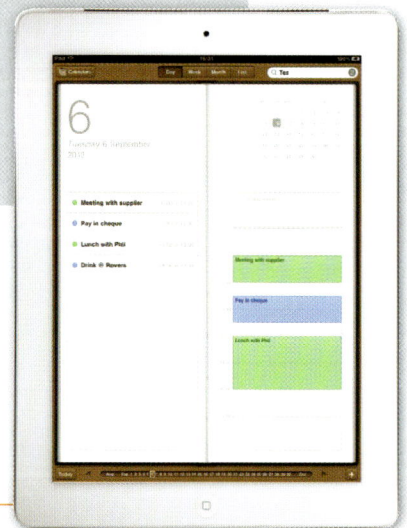

The main event

Here's your main Calendar interface, in Month view. You can change how you view your calendar using these buttons at the centre-top of the screen.

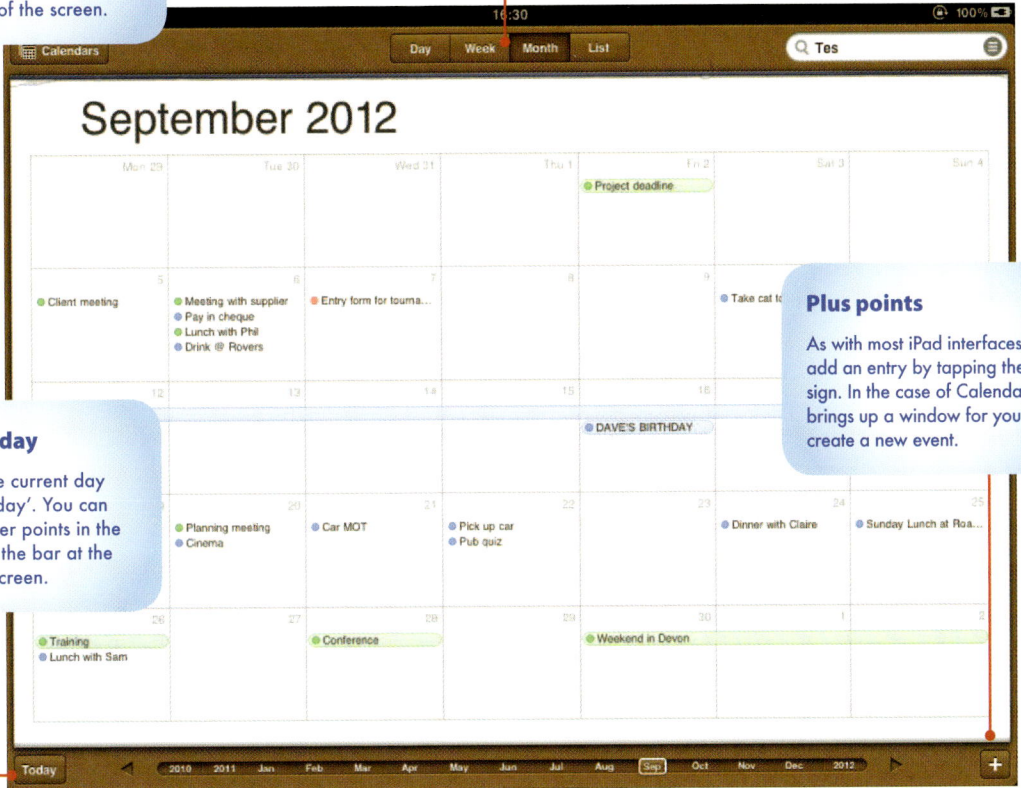

Today's the day

Skip to view the current day by tapping 'Today'. You can also skip to other points in the calendar using the bar at the bottom of the screen.

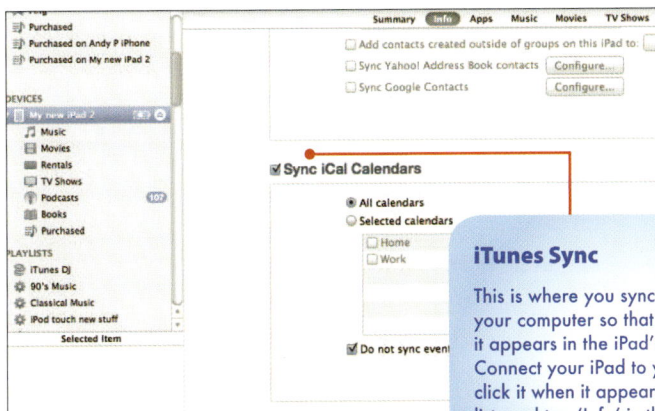

Plus points

As with most iPad interfaces, you add an entry by tapping the '+' sign. In the case of Calendar, this brings up a window for you to create a new event.

16:30 100%

| | Day | Week | Month | List | | Q Tes |

September 2012

Mon 29	Tue 30	Wed 31	Thu 1	Fri 2	Sat 3	Sun 4
				Project deadline		

| 5 | 6 | 7 | 8 | 9 | | |
| Client meeting | Meeting with supplier / Pay in cheque / Lunch with Phil / Drink @ Rovers | Entry form for tourna... | | Take cat to | | |

| 12 | 13 | 14 | 15 | 16 | | |
| | | | DAVE'S BIRTHDAY | | | |

| | 20 | 21 | 22 | 23 | 24 | 25 |
| Planning meeting / Cinema | Car MOT | Pick up car / Pub quiz | | Dinner with Claire | Sunday Lunch at Roa... | |

| 26 | 27 | 28 | 29 | 30 | 1 | 2 |
| Training / Lunch with Sam | Conference | | Weekend in Devon | | | |

Today ◄ 2010 2011 Jan Feb Mar Apr May Jun Jul Aug Sep Oct Nov Dec 2012 ► +

| | Summary | Info | Apps | Music | Movies | TV Shows |

Purchased
Purchased on Andy P iPhone
Purchased on My new iPad 2

DEVICES
My new iPad 2
  Music
  Movies
  Rentals
  TV Shows
  Podcasts
  Books
  Purchased
PLAYLISTS
  iTunes DJ
  90's Music
  Classical Music
  iPod touch new stuff
  Selected Item

Add contacts created outside of groups on this iPad to:
☐ Sync Yahoo! Address Book contacts   Configure...
☐ Sync Google Contacts   Configure...

☑ Sync iCal Calendars
  ○ All calendars
  ○ Selected calendars
    ☐ Home
    ☐ Work

☑ Do not sync event

iTunes Sync

This is where you sync a calendar from your computer so that the information in it appears in the iPad's Calendar app. Connect your iPad to your computer, click it when it appears in the source list, and tap 'Info' in the bar at the top of the screen. Scroll down to 'Sync iCal Calendars' and tick this box (this is on a Mac; on a PC you'll have the option to sync from Outlook).

EXPERT TIP

Even the Calendar's icon on your home screen has some neat functionality built in – it updates every day, so it always displays today's date.

Step-by-step guide ⟩⟩⟩

Using Calendar

Get to grips with the elegant Calendar app, and you'll never need to turn to a paper diary ever again. Here are six steps to managing your appointments on your iPad.

1 When you first fire up Calendar it will present you with Day view. This is ideal for busy people as it presents you with an hour-by-hour view of what you need to do and where you need to be.

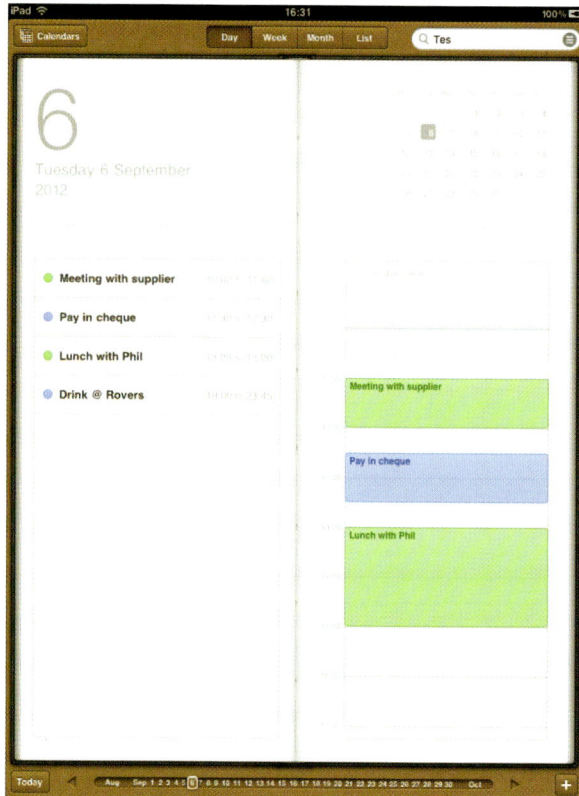

2 Month and Week views are pretty self-explanatory, but the List view gives you a kitchen calendar-style summary of your appointments on the left, and a regular Day view on the right – great for a quick overview of your commitments.

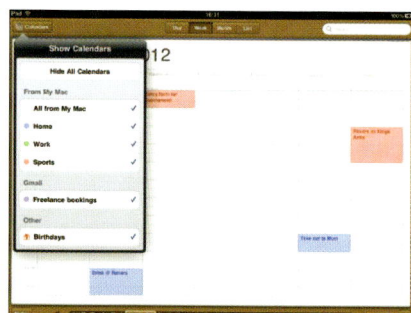

3 Tap 'Calendars' in the top-left to bring up a list of your calendars. You can set up calendars for home, work or your team's sports fixtures, for example. Tap the calendars in the list to toggle them to visible or invisible.

NEED TO KNOW Time zones

If you're setting alerts and events for when you are travelling, you will want your alerts to appear at your destination's local time. To make that happen, open the Settings app, and go to Mail, Contacts, Calendars. Scroll down to 'Calendars' and you'll see an option to set your time zone.

4 Tap 'Search' in the top-right to scan your calendars for events – handy if you can't for the life of you remember when somebody's birthday is. Results appear in a pop-up; tap a search result to skip right to it.

WANT MORE?
CalenGoo

If Calendar's Google Calendar support doesn't cut it for you, try the £2.99 CalenGoo app. It's not as good-looking as the built-in Calendar, but it does sync with your online Google Calendar every time you open the app.

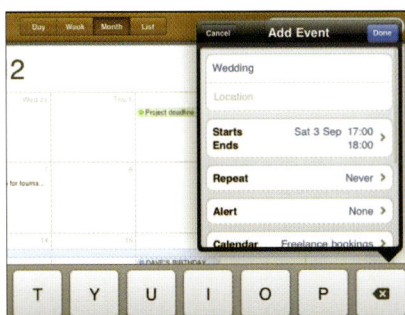

5 Tap the '+' sign to add an event. Use the on-screen keyboard to enter the event's details. Remember to set a 'Repeat' if it's a recurring appointment, and enter an alert time if you need a reminder.

6 Tap the time in the event creator window to set the time. You also have the option to set an event as 'All-day'. When you've finished entering your event, tap 'Done' on the pop up window and it will appear in your Calendar.

Photo fun with the iPad's cameras

▶ Unlike the original iPad, the iPad 2 came with front and rear-facing cameras. The new iPad ups the ante still further, upgrading its rear-facing lens to a 5-megapixel iSight camera that's capable of capturing Full HD video. To help you make the most of them, the iPad 2 and new iPad both come with three camera-based apps: Camera, Photo Booth, and FaceTime.

The last of these is a big draw. Video chat using the new iPad's lovely screen is a great feature, and FaceTime works very well indeed. It's a WiFi-only feature, though.

Photo Booth is a webcam app that allows you to take pictures with the iPad's front-facing camera, as well as letting you apply cool and funny effects to your self-portraits or pictures of the outside world taken with the iPad's rear-facing camera.

The Camera app lets you take pictures and video using either of the two lenses. Here's your guided tour of each app.

VITAL INFO

This tutorial shows you how to use the iPad's built-in camera apps, Camera, Photo Booth and FaceTime.

What you need
Your new iPad or iPad 2
Your best smile

Time required
1 hour

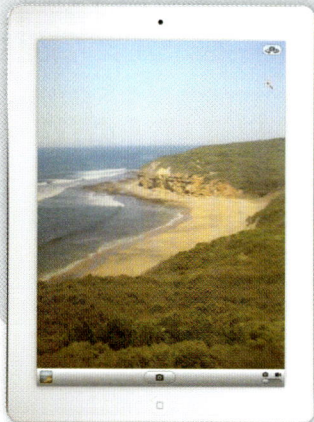

Special effects

Fire up Photo Booth and you'll see this screen (after the red curtain animation has swooped past the display, that is). This allows you to pick your effect.

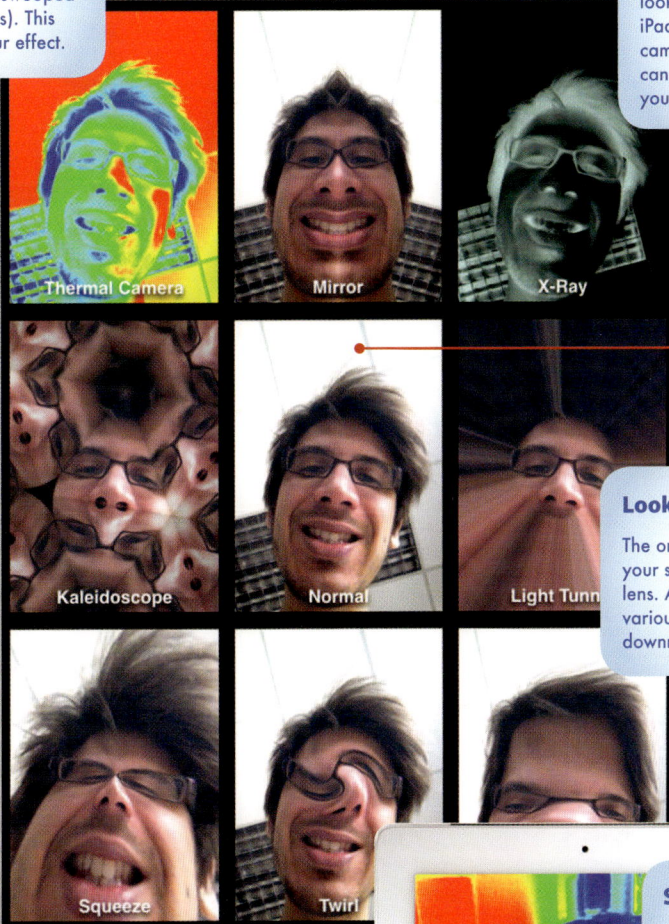

Camera lens

Here's the camera lens that looks at you as you look at your iPad 2 or new iPad. The other camera is on the back – you can switch between them once you've picked your effect.

Look at me

The one in the middle is your straightforward camera lens. All the others give you various creative, spooky, and downright silly effects.

Shutter button

Once you've picked your effect you'll be taken to the main camera screen, where you can take a picture using the shutter button at the bottom-centre of the screen.

Choose another

Press this button to be taken back to the previous screen and choose another effect.

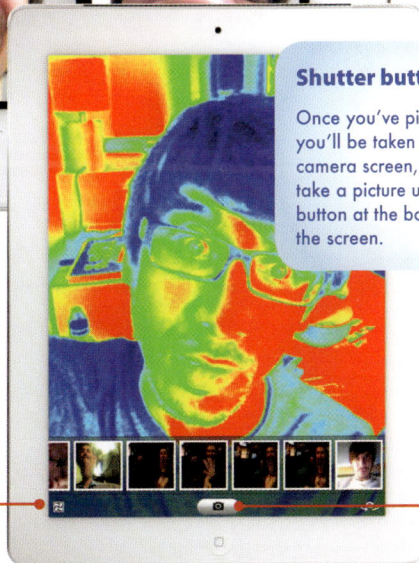

Thermal Camera

Mirror

X-Ray

Kaleidoscope

Normal

Light Tunn

Squeeze

Twirl

Step-by-step guide ❯❯❯

Lights, Camera, action!

The Camera app is a little more serious than Photo Booth. It lets you take photos
and videos, which you can edit on the iPad using apps like Apple's incredible iMovie.

WANT MORE?
Shot focus
In Video mode, you can edit the area of focus while you shoot. Just tap a different part of the screen to change the focal point of the shot.

1 Fire up the Camera and this is what you'll see. By default it will use the rear-facing camera and it will be set to take still shots. Press the 'Shutter' button – in the middle at the bottom of the screen – to take a picture.

2 Both lenses have 'tap to focus' features. This means you can tap anywhere on the screen to focus the lens – this allows you to take shots that are a little more creative. Tap a second time to change focus.

3 The toggle switch on the bottom-right of the screen lets you swap between video shooting and still shooting. Tap it and the shutter button becomes a red 'Record' button. Tap to focus works in video mode, too.

WANT MORE?
Learn iMovie

Turn to **page 136** for your four-page guide on how to edit your videos wherever you are using Apple's iMovie filmmaking app.

4 Switch the lenses by tapping the icon in the top-right of the screen. Just as it does in Photo Booth, the screen will animate to show you it's flipping the view from the rear-facing camera to the front-facing camera.

5 To view the pictures you've taken, tap the square in the bottom-left of the screen. This will take you to the last picture or video that you took. You can swipe left or right on the screen to view your images.

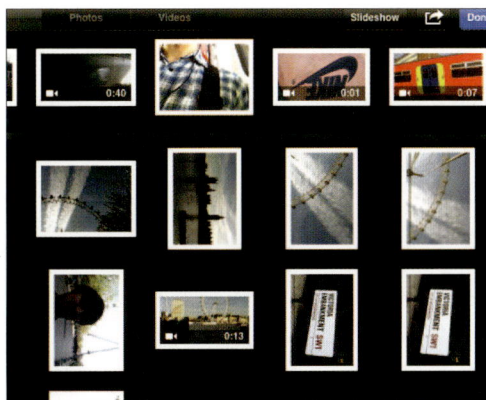

6 Alternatively, tap 'Camera Roll' in the top-left of your screen to view shots as thumbnails. Tap the arrow icon (top-right) and then tap image thumbnails to select images to be emailed, copied, printed, or deleted.

FaceTime your friends

The other headline feature offered by the front-facing cameras on the iPad 2 and new iPad is FaceTime video calling. It's an incredibly impressive system – and here's how to do it. Make sure you're connected to WiFi and see who's online.

When you first use FaceTime, you'll need to register your email address. Follow the onscreen instructions – you'll need your Apple ID that you use on the iTunes Store.

1 iPhone 4 phone numbers are automatically recognised in FaceTime, you just have to turn it on in Settings > Phone. Here's our contacts book – this contact has an iPhone 4, and so his record appears with a FaceTime button. Press it to FaceTime call straight from the Contacts app.

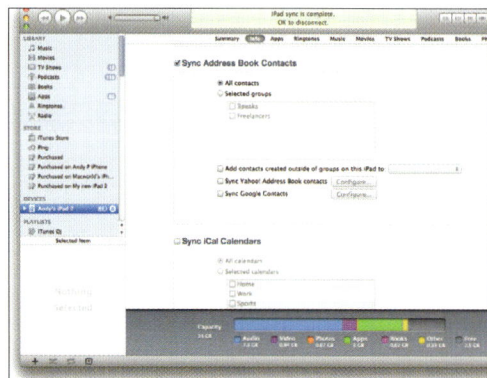

2 Your FaceTime contacts are set up automatically, so it's a good idea to have your contacts on your computer on Mail or Outlook and sync your contacts book from iTunes. Do this on the 'Info' page on the sync screen when your iPad is plugged in.

3 Back on your iPad – starting the FaceTime app turns on the front camera and shows you a full list of contacts. If you try to call a non-FaceTime contact it won't work – you can only call people on an iPhone 4, Mac, iPod Touch or iPad.

To test FaceTime's mettle, we called a friend who was using a WiFi connection in a bar in Internet-restricted Beijing, China. It looked very blurry, but it connected first time!

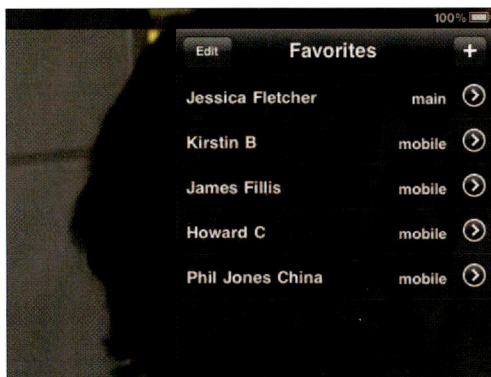

4 As not all of your contacts will have compatible devices, it's a good idea to add those that do to your 'Favorites'. To do that, simply tap on a contact and tap 'Add To Favorites'. That way all your FaceTime friends will be in one place.

5 Tap a phone number or email address on a contact entry (or simply tap their name if the contact is in your 'Favorites'), and you'll be connected. It makes a peeping sound while it connects, and can take a while.

6 And there you have it – free video chatting over WiFi. Tap the camera-flip icon to show your friend what you're looking at – great for sharing with your friend when you've got a load of people in the room. To hang up, press 'End'.

Explore the Internet with Safari

▶ When Apple launched its first touchscreen device, the original iPhone, the mobile web browser was the feature that really blew people away. It was the first time true representations had appeared on a mobile web browser, and the new iPad is the best device so far for mobile viewing of web pages.

The new hardware helps – web browsing is faster than ever thanks to the dual-core A5X chip, and web content is crystal clear, courtesy of the new iPad's high-resolution Retina display. Browsing the Internet on the iPad is one of the device's key functions – so fire up Safari and get started.

VITAL INFO

We show you around the Safari browser – the most complete mobile web browser out there. Browse the Internet and personalise the app so you can access your favourite sites within a few taps.

What you need
Your iPad
A WiFi Internet connection – or 3G/4G Internet connection if you have a new iPad WiFi + 4G model, or earlier 3G iPad

Time required
20 minutes

Set up WiFi

If you're on a new iPad 4G model, or the 3G versions of the earlier iPads, you should be on the Internet as long as your SIM card is inserted. To connect to WiFi instead, go to Settings and tap General > Network.

Choose your network

Tap 'WiFi' and you'll see a list of available WiFi networks. Tap one to join it. Most WiFi is locked these days, so you'll need to log in with the password. If you're at home, this is the same password you use on your computer.

WANT MORE?
360 Web Browser

If Safari is not to your taste, why not try 360 Web Browser (59p)? It's an app that offers a different browsing experience, as well as a Download Manager and Firefox syncing. It's available through the App Store.

Explore the Internet

The Internet on an iPad looks just like it does on your computer. Tap either the 'Google' box or the main URL box in the taskbar to enter a site you already know.

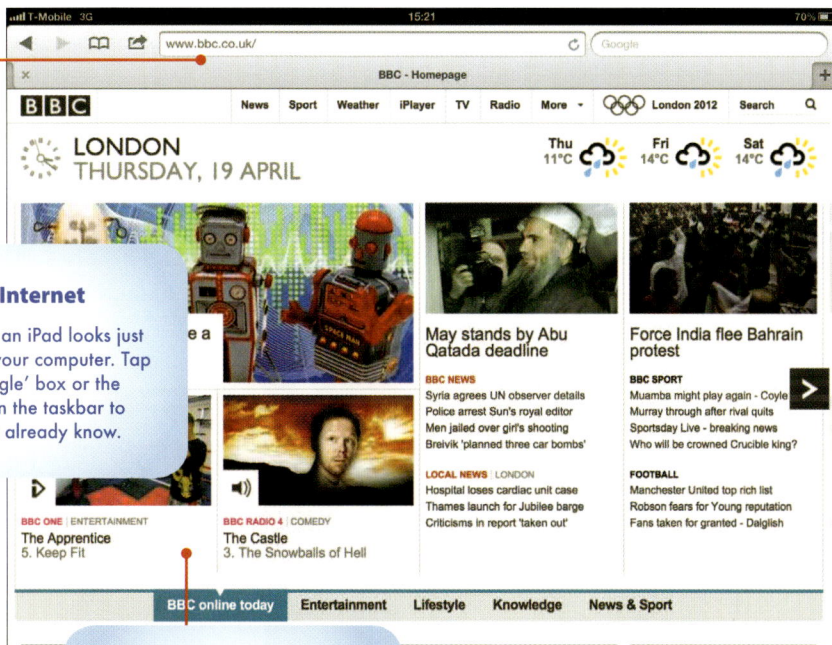

Touch navigation

Double-tap a column of text or a picture on a page to zoom in so the item fills your screen. You can also zoom in and out by pinching and stretching your fingers on the screen.

Step-by-step guide ⟫⟫

1 Fire up Safari for the first time and you'll see a blank page. Tap the URL bar to enter the address of a website to visit. Or use the Search bar (which is marked Google by default) to search for something.

2 Tap links to navigate to them. Tap and hold a link to see options to open it in a new page or copy the URL for pasting elsewhere. You can also tap and hold pictures to copy or save the image to your Photos library.

WANT MORE?
Search preferences

In Settings > Safari > Search engine, you can choose between using Google, Yahoo!, or Bing as your default option in Safari's Search bar.

3 To open a new tab, tap the icon in the top bar that looks like one square laid over another. Then pick 'New Page'. Tap this icon at any time to navigate between your various open pages.

4 To bookmark a page, tap the arrow icon at the top and tap 'Add Bookmark'. Once you've got some set up, tap the open book icon to navigate between your bookmarks.

5 You can also set up a web bookmark on your home screen. To do this, tap the arrow icon then tap 'Add to Home Screen'. Name the bookmark, and hit 'Add'. The icon will appear on your Home Screen.

6 Finally, you can email a link to a friend from within Safari. Hit the arrow, then 'Mail Link to this Page'. This will create an email message from within Safari – type a custom message if you wish and hit 'Send'.

Using the iPod app to play media

▶ The iPod changed music listening. Now it's an app inside every iOS device, including your iPad. The app gives you all the tools you need for music, podcast and audiobook listening. It features a search function that lets you find your music fast, and Apple's powerful AirPlay system that lets you output your music via an Apple TV, AirPort Express-connected home stereo system or any AirPlay-capable device. Simple controls make your iPad's iPod app easy to use. There are five music categories for easy navigation of your media: Songs, Artists, Albums, Genres, and Composers. The amazing Genius function puts together music playback sessions for you. And you can flip through your full-size album art just as you would flip through CDs – it's great, and Home Sharing brings even more music to you.

VITAL INFO

We're going to help you make and edit playlists on your iPad, and show you how to power-manage music playback in full-screen view.

What you need:
Your iPad
iPod app
PC/Mac with iTunes collection
WiFi network

Time required
10 minutes

Music menu

All your media is accessed via the left-hand Library menu. Here you can access your podcasts, audiobooks, music and playlists.

Find music fast

In a hurry? No problem: just tap the artist name, song title, album name or composer into the search bar here for instant results.

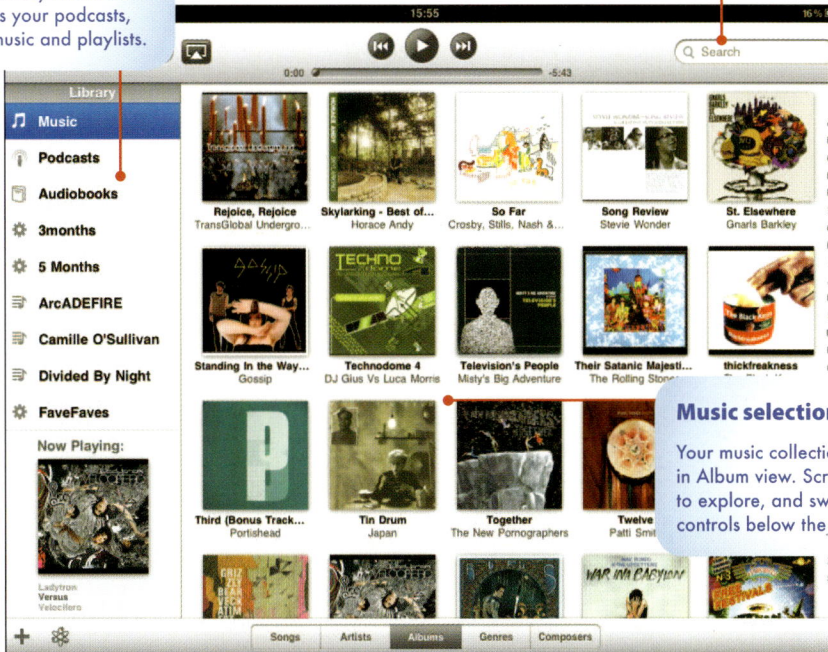

Music selection

Your music collection looks like this in Album view. Scroll up and down to explore, and swap views using the controls below the collection.

Sight return

Tap the left-facing arrow to leave full-screen view and return to the main menu, for example when selecting the next track.

Track control

Here you can tell iTunes to randomly play tracks, run through music sequentially, and keep an eye on how much longer the current track will play.

Track listing

This button, when tapped, gives you a list of all the tracks on the album you are currently playing, so you can switch to another song as you please.

Genius is what it says on the can. Apple's recommendation technology will create a playlist based on your current track, just tap the icon that looks like an atom. To save a playlist? Tap the 'Save' icon.

Media studies

Tap to choose, tap to play, swipe to navigate and play your music using your headphones, Bluetooth headphones, AirPort Express or an AirPlay system – iTunes on the iPad is a great way to listen to music. Now we're going to help you get familiar with the app using some of its extra tools.

1 Playlists are selections of tracks that you think work well together. You can use your iPad to create these. To start a new list, click the '+' icon at the bottom left of the screen, you'll be asked to name the playlist.

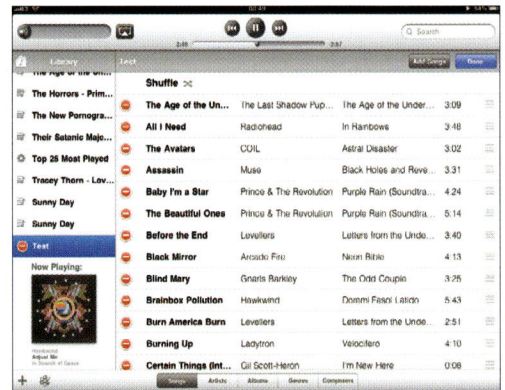

2 Once you've named your playlist, the next window lets you add songs to the list. As songs are added they grey out. Tap the Sources button to access podcasts and songs from other playlists. Tap 'Done' when you're finished.

3 When you've finished you'll have your own lovingly-crafted collection of tracks. You can add new songs and edit existing lists by selecting them and tapping the 'Edit' button. Remove tracks by tapping the Red button by track name in Edit view.

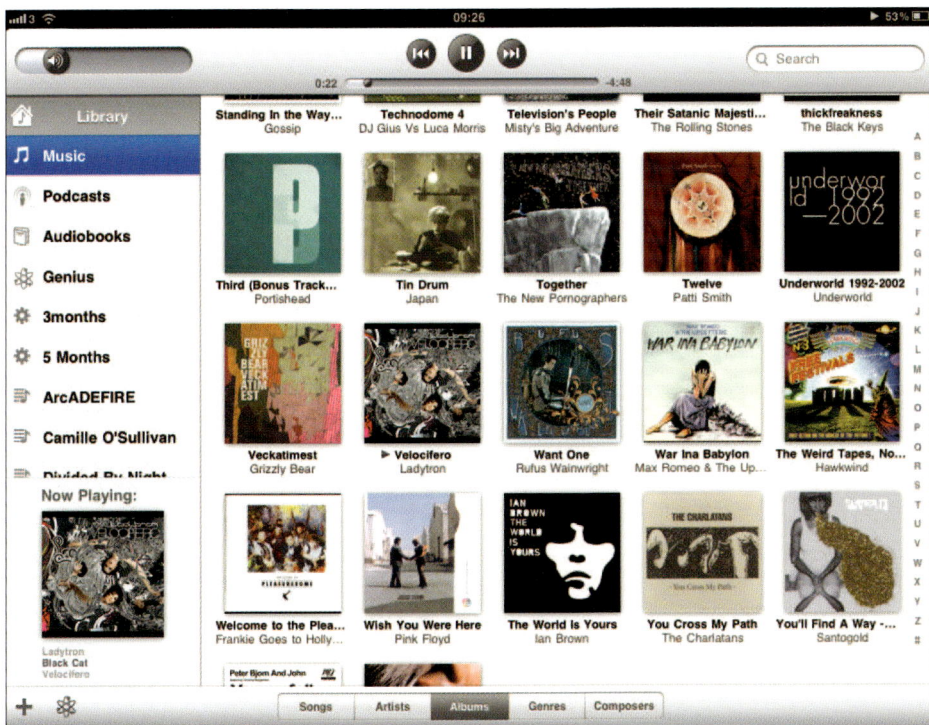

WANT MORE?
Shazam

If you love music you'll love Shazam, which lets you use your iPad to identify any music you hear playing as you go – an iPad essential.

4 When you have music playing, the relevant album cover shows in the lower-left box. Tap on the box and you'll get a full-screen view. Tap once on this and the command menu overlay appears, with a series of commands you can use.

5 Most of the commands are self-explanatory, but those in the narrow strip underneath the track name are worth exploring. Tap on the squiggly arrows to the right and your album or playlist plays in random order. Tap it again to return to sequential order.

6 To the left of the narrow strip is another arrow icon. Tap this to set your track up to repeat. Tap it again to switch repeat off. Tap the lower right icon to enter album track view, which displays and lets you tap to play any of the tracks in the current album.

Get extra storage with iCloud

▶ Your iPad comes with 16GB, 32GB or 64GB of internal storage. iCloud allows you to extend the amount of storage available, taking advantage of Apple's remote servers. You can then access content that you've saved to iCloud via either 3G or WiFi.

Apple offers 5GB of free iCloud storage but charges an annual fee for higher storage amounts. The benefit of iCloud is that it connects compatible Apple products such as a MacBook, Apple TV and iPhone and shares content on all devices. Read a book on your iPhone, and you can continue reading on your iPad from the same page. Similarly, your Photo Stream can be viewed on all devices – even your telly, if you own an Apple TV.

VITAL INFO

iCloud is the online storage service offered by Apple. Your mail, calendar, photos and more are all stored remotely and backed up every day by Apple.

What you need:
Your iPad or any iCloud-compatible device

Time required
5 minutes

Pricing

5GB is the default amount of iCloud storage that you get for free. There are three further capacity sizes that require an annual subscription. You can purchase extra storage through the Settings > iCloud menu.

The tariff is as follows...

10GB iCloud Storage - £14 a year

20GB iCloud Storage - £28 a year

50GB iCloud Storage - £70 a year

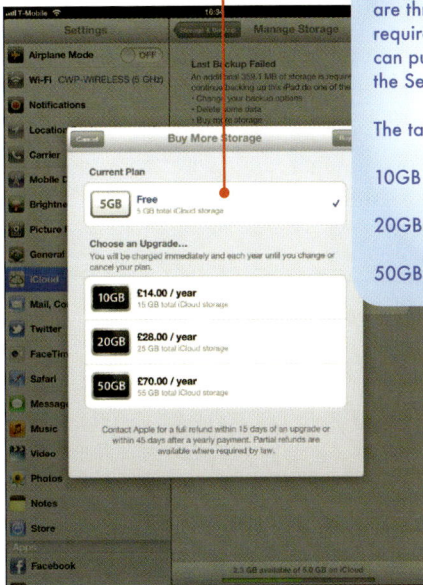

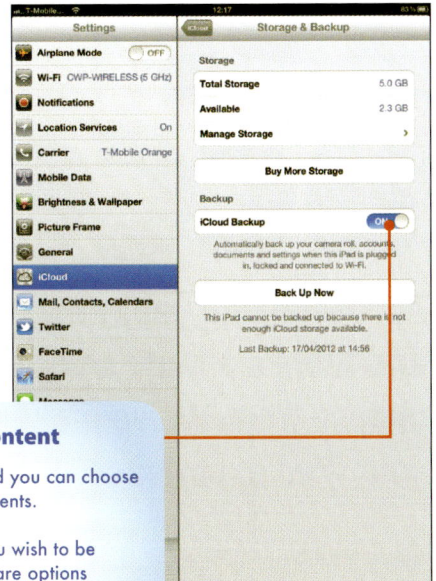

How to back up your content

Head to Settings > iCloud and you can choose to instantly back up your contents.

You can also choose what you wish to be backed up via iCloud. There are options to turn backup on or off for mail, contacts, calendars, reminders, bookmarks, notes, Photo Stream, documents and data. To sync and back up your Notes, you'll need to create a free @me.com email address via Apple.

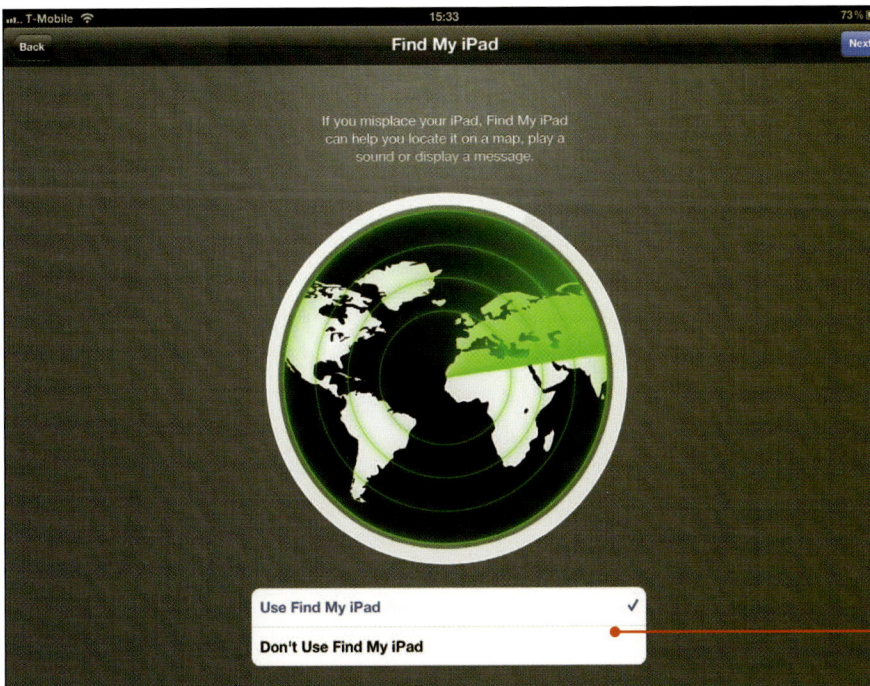

Find My iPad

If you lose your iPad, iCloud allows you to locate your tablet on a map and remotely delete all sensitive data and lock the device so that it can no longer be used.

Head to Settings > iCloud and slide the Find My iPad button to On.

Top 25 iPad accessories

Accessorising your new iPad is half the fun of buying one, and there's a huge selection of gadgets, gizmos and add-ons to choose from. We've picked 25 of the best accessories to boost your iPad experience.

Apple iPad Smart Cover

www.store.apple.com/uk
Polyurethane – £35
Leather - £59

The Smart Cover is one of those ridiculously clever ideas that only Apple could come up with. The magnetic hinges on the cover automatically line up with the edges of the iPad, while the segmented panels on the cover allow it to fold up and act as a stand.

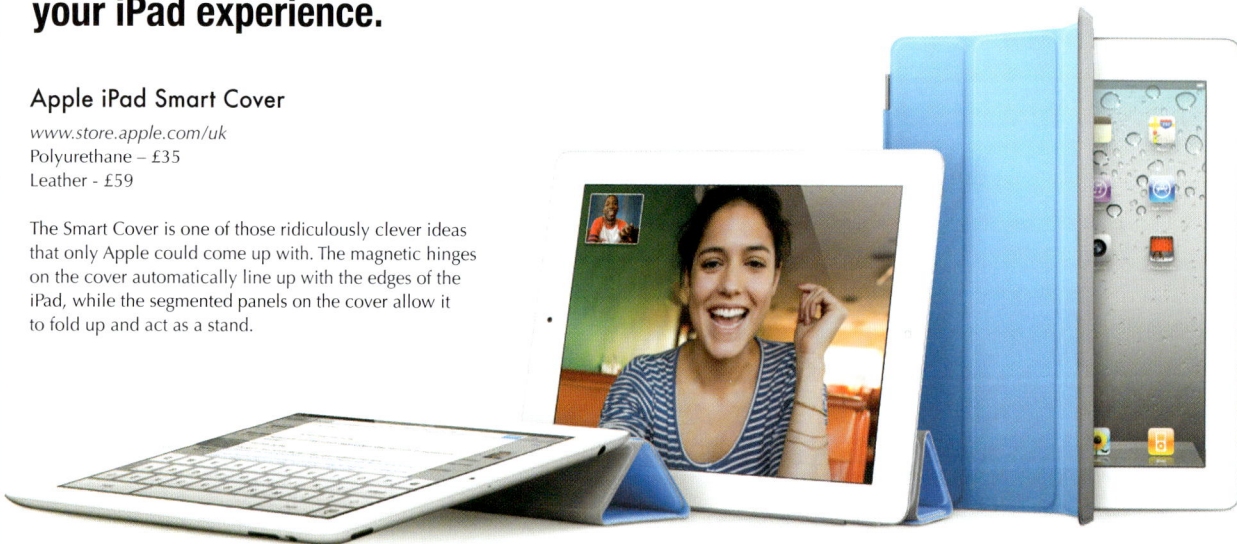

Air Speaker

www.loewe.tv/uk
£649

So you've heard about Apple AirPlay, and fancy streaming music directly from your iPhone to a music system? Tech expert Loewe has created the Air Speaker, a discreet yet chunky speaker that pumps out 80 Watts of power through two subwoofers, two tweeters and two mid-range speakers. What does all that mean? It sounds brilliant wherever you choose to use it. The only downside is the price – as one of the first 'flagship' AirPlay speakers, it's got a big price tag.

Sennheiser MM50-X Travel

www.sennheiser.co.uk
£349

The MM50-X headphones are the best Bluetooth headphones around. There are buttons for selecting tracks, adjusting volume and taking voice calls on the cups. Once paired, you can be truly wireless – they also cut out external noise using NoiseGard 2.0 tech, so commuter heaven awaits...

Apple iPad Camera Connection Kit

Apple
www.store.apple.com/uk
£25

Compatible with both versions of the iPad, the Camera Connection Kit consists of two components. A USB adaptor allows you to connect your camera directly to the iPad in order to transfer your photos, or you can use the memory card reader to insert a memory card instead.

Seagate GoFlex Satellite

www.seagate.com
£169

Watching movies or storing loads of photos or music on a 16GB iPad can be an issue. The GoFlex Satellite solves this problem by acting as a wireless hard drive with a massive 500GB of storage for files. Impressively, it can stream three HD movies to different iDevices simultaneously and without a power source (after charging), so you can store it in your bag and access it whenever you want.

Apple Digital AV Adapter

Apple
www.store.apple.com/uk
£35

At long last – the Digital AV Adapter provides an HDMI interface so that you can hook your iPad up to a flat-screen HD TV – and it also works with the current iPhone and iPod Touch. Apple makes similar adaptors with VGA output for computer monitors, as well as composite and component video.

Apple Wireless Keyboard

www.store.apple.com/uk
£57

The iPad's on-screen keyboard is fine for bashing out a quick email, but if you want to knock up something more substantial, a physical keyboard comes in very handy. This Bluetooth Wireless Keyboard is a good choice if you want a proper keyboard for typing on the iPad. It's slim, light and very portable.

Pipetto Hunter Wanderer

www.pipetto.co.uk
£99

Not content with dominating the fashion welly market, Hunter has produced a very smart iPad carry case. The outside is made of waterproof waxed cotton, there's a handy carry handle and – as with the Apple Smart Covers – the Hunter Wanderer sends your iPad to sleep when you close the cover. The whole case acts as a stand, can be attached to the rear of a car headrest, and offers the best protection available for your iPad. It's expensive but worth it.

Monitor Audio iDeck 200

www.monitoraudio.co.uk
£249

The Monitor Audio iDeck 200 is a great quality dock for iPhone and iPad that offers style, performance and loud volumes – all without breaking a sweat. The sound is easily capable of filling a large room, thanks to the iDeck 200's custom-designed dual 50W bass drivers and 20W tweeters.

Zeppelin Air

www.bowers-wilkins.co.uk
£499

The original Zeppelin speaker got rave reviews, and the Zeppelin Air is one of the first of a new generation of speaker systems equipped with Apple's wireless AirPlay technology. AirPlay transmits audio using WiFi – rather than Bluetooth – and a lossless audio format that provides top quality for your music. Your friends and family will definitely stop and stare...

Touchscreen Gloves

www.monsterstuff.co.uk
£7.99

Want to use your iPad but keep your gloves on? You can – as long as you don't mind the silver tips on these fingers which allow you to swipe and type as you would without gloves. They aren't the thickest of gloves, but work flawlessly with your iPad and are a bit of a bargain.

Vogel Ringo

www.tabletonthewall.com
£69.99

By allowing you to stick your iPad on the wall, the Vogel Ringo turns your tablet into a TV for the kitchen or deluxe jukebox screen for AirPlay fun with your compatible AirPlay hi-fi or dock. It's sturdy and it even works well in the car, making for stress-free journeys. A great gadget that all the family can use.

Phiaton PS 500 headphones

www.iheadphones.co.uk
£169.99

Designed for home use, the Phiaton PS 500 headphones look like they mean business. The giant ear cushions, thick black surround and heavy headband are extremely rugged, before you consider the external croc skin-style finish. In use, the Phiaton PS 500s feel comfy and can fit the largest of heads. Sound is great for the money and there's a fabric cord which means less tangles too. They're an ideal companion for iPad gaming, movies or music use.

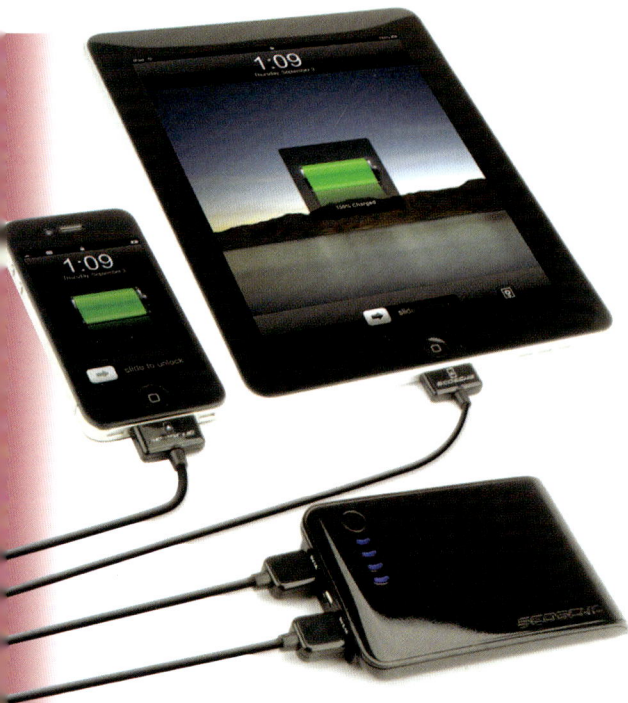

goBAT II

www.scosche.com
£79.99

The goBATT II is a compact little battery pack that you can easily slip into your pocket when you're out and about. It can charge an iPad to 50 per cent of a full charge, providing up to six hours of additional use. It's equipped with two separate USB ports, allowing you to charge an iPhone at the same time and is a good option for travellers away from a power source.

Arcam drDock

www.arcam.co.uk
£200

If you want to connect your iPad to a hi-fi or any amplifier, this is a superb dock. Better still, it has an HDMI output so you can watch your 1080p movies on the big screen and have an iPad as the centre of your home entertainment system without needing an Apple TV.

Amphion NuForce Helium 410

www.amphion.nl
£950

This micro audio set-up is designed for desktop use, and that little box with knobs on is an amplifier, ready to suck sounds from your iPad and pump them out through the Amphion speakers, custom-built to be enjoyed at close quarters. Expensive compared to AirPlay docks but, well, just look at it. The speakers are truly high-end hi-fi quality too, if your budget can stretch to this system...

iPad Shine Case

www.proporta.com
£49.95

Want to make your iPad look just like a handbag?
The Shine Case does exactly that and even includes
a screen print and neat magnetic closing lock. There's
a pouch for paper notes inside, even though Apple
has previously said that "iPad is replacing pen and
paper all over the world". If you're still living in a
dual world of iPad and paper, it's a smart buy. Certainly
beats stuffing notes into the back of your Smart Cover.

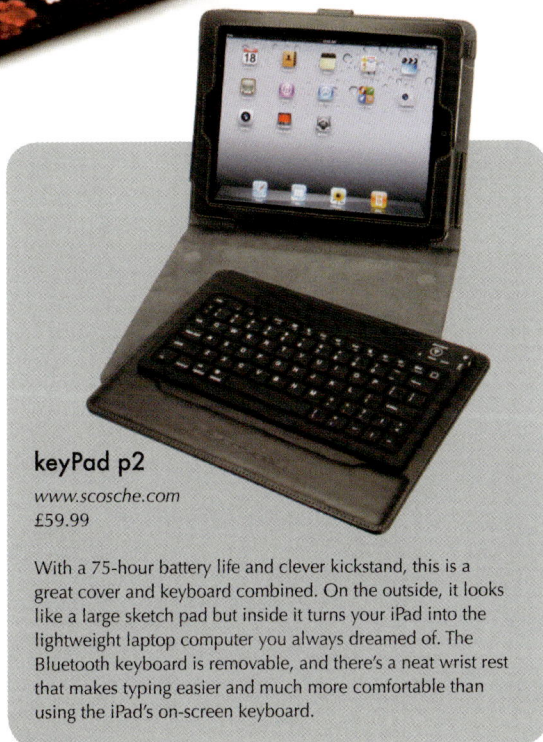

keyPad p2

www.scosche.com
£59.99

With a 75-hour battery life and clever kickstand, this is a
great cover and keyboard combined. On the outside, it looks
like a large sketch pad but inside it turns your iPad into the
lightweight laptop computer you always dreamed of. The
Bluetooth keyboard is removable, and there's a neat wrist rest
that makes typing easier and much more comfortable than
using the iPad's on-screen keyboard.

Kensington PowerBolt Duo

www.eu.kensington.com
£24.99

The iPad's battery should last even through long motorway
journeys, but it's worth having a car charger just in case.
Several companies make these, but Kensington's PowerBolt
Duo has two USB ports, allowing you to charge an
iPad and an iPhone or another device at the same time.
Perfect for avoiding arguments on those long road trips...

Maroo Otago

www.maroo.com
£54.99

If you're an iPad user with an Apple wireless keyboard, the chances are you're going to need a case to accompany your iPad Smart Cover. The Otago is a protective leather case that screams business and forms a stand so you can type in comfort. It's expensive (as much as an Apple keyboard) but if you're using an iPad as a laptop replacement on the go, it certainly looks the part and will inspire instant intrigue from fellow commuters – if you're on a train with a table, of course.

Sony XA900iP

www.Sony.co.uk
£499

Snapping at the heels of speaker style experts Bowers & Wilkins' Zeppelin dock and the ultra high-end DA-E750 dock from Samsung, the XA900iP is Sony admitting that no, you don't always need a Sony micro system to get great sound. Packing Bluetooth, Airplay and serious power, it's a giant dock capable of filling the largest room with decent sound. It looks great alongside an iPad, naturally, and is an exciting development for Sony as the Japanese company focuses on high-end phone and tablet accessories in 2012.

StompBox

www.griffintechnology.com
£69.95

Another great gadget for musicians, the StompBox is a four-channel effects pedalboard that's compatible with any iOS device, but works best on iPad. It was designed to work with the popular iShred guitar amp app, and includes a cable for connecting a guitar, and a standard input jack for connecting other devices. It's ideal for budding musicians.

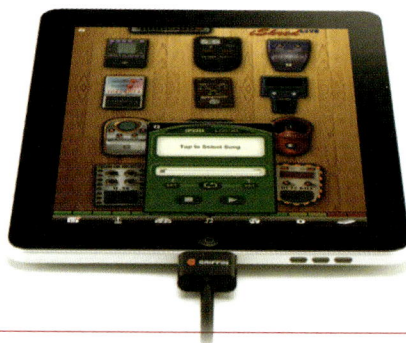

Griffin Beacon Remote

www.griffin.com
£59.99

Turn your iPad into a remote control and programme planner for all your TV and subscription TV services. Download the Dijit app and you can browse channels and connect to any remote control device in your home from TV to Hi-Fi to Sky, set-top box or Freesat recorder.

Vodafone R201

www.vodafone.co.uk
£30 (12 month Vodafone contract, at £15 per month)

The R201 is a rechargeable, portable internet hot spot, allowing five devices to connect to it just like a regular home Wi-Fi network. £15 a month gets you 2GB of data – which isn't bad – and European data top-ups are cheap at £2 per day, based on 25MB of data use a day. It's small enough to fit in a jacket pocket too.

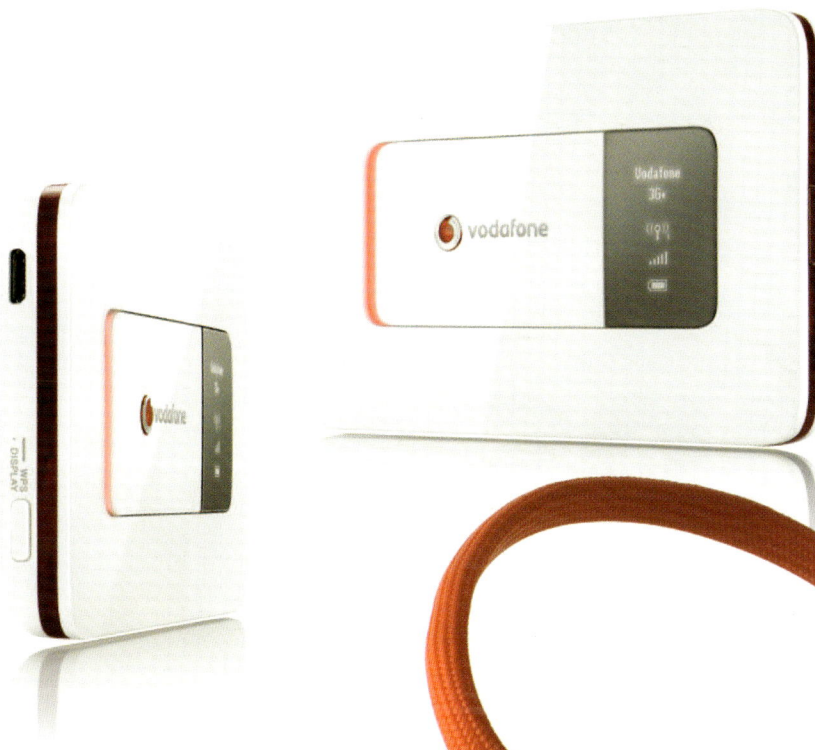

WeSC Banjo headphones

www.iheadphones.co.uk
£39.99

Fashionable over-ear headphones for those that prefer a tight fit and loud colours. The Banjo's 40mm drivers to deliver decent enough sound for their budget price.

The 50 best iPad apps

Forget trawling the App Store for the good stuff – just read this definitive top 50

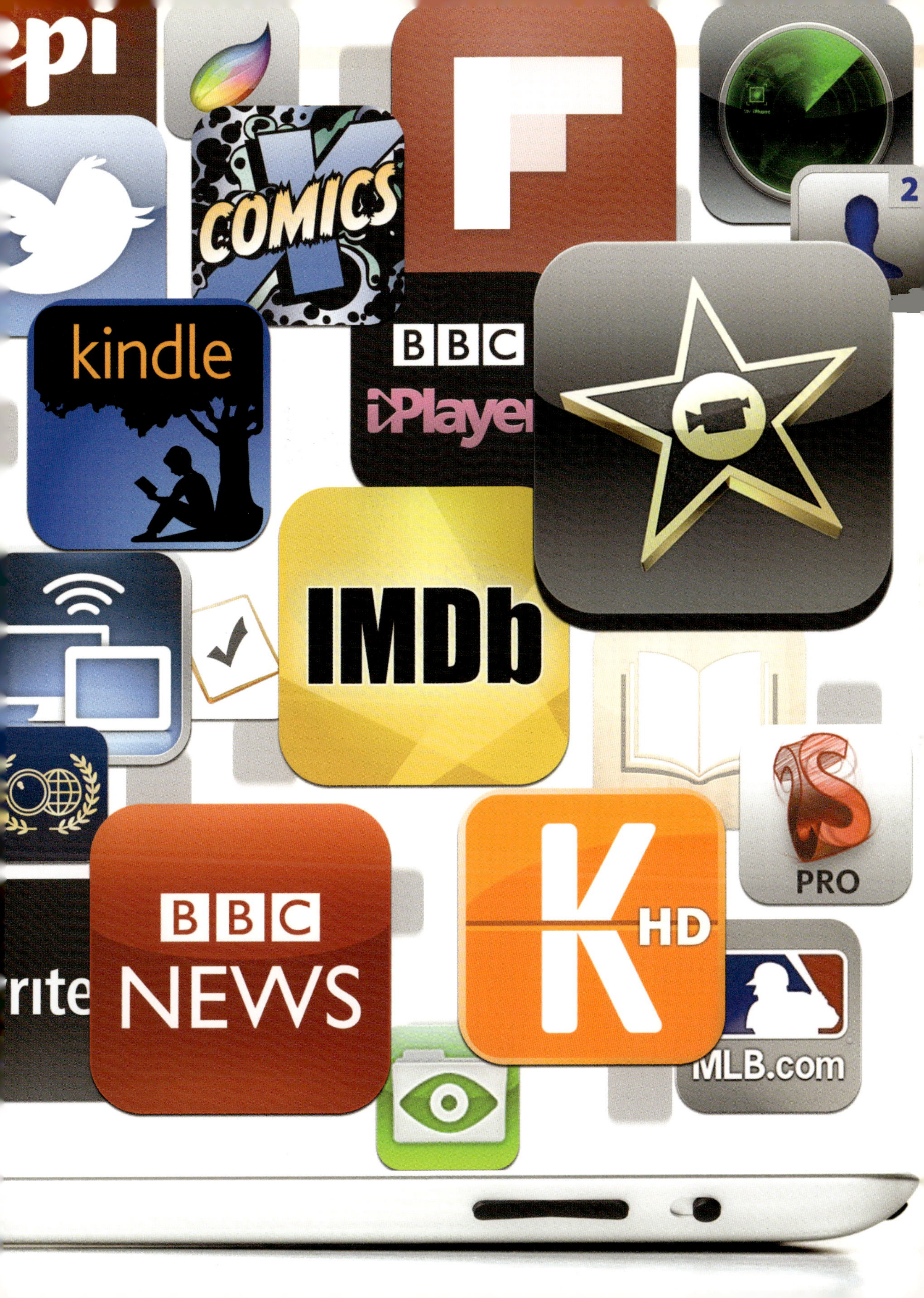
COMICS
kindle
BBC
IMDb
BBC
NEWS
HD
PRO
MLB.com

GarageBand
£2.99

Even if you've never played so much as a tambourine, GarageBand for iPad lets you compose and record your musical masterpiece. With a complete set of Smart Instruments at your disposal, GarageBand provides the simplest way for wannabe maestros to put together professional-sounding songs in seconds. Experienced musicians can plug in real instruments, play virtual keys and strings, and record their work.

See Apps in depth, page 108

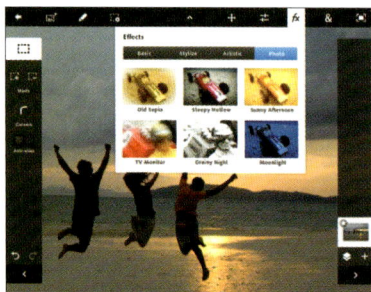

Adobe Photoshop Touch
£6.99

The iPad version of Adobe's premier desktop image editor includes many of the most popular features of its big brother, and can share work with it – good for working on an image on the go and then importing it to the desktop.

Reeder for iPad
£2.99

If you use Google Reader, Reeder for iPad might just be your best choice for viewing its contents on your tablet. The app syncs with your account and offers a beautiful interface for you to browse your feeds.

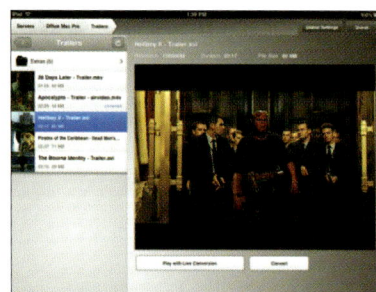

Air Video
£1.79

If you use an iPad you'll know how annoying it can be when you have movies that aren't in the correct format. Air Video lets you stream movies in almost any format from your computer to your iPad, converting them on the fly, even over 3G!

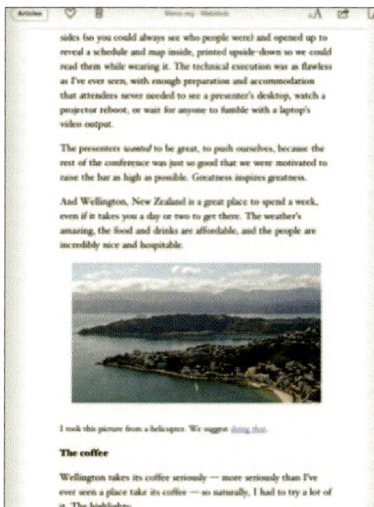

Instapaper
£2.99

How often do you see an article online that you want to read but you don't have the time? If this is a familiar scenario, Instapaper is your answer. Store posts and news stories for later within a smooth interface that makes reading even better than the original document.

iMovie
£2.99

Making movies isn't the niche skill it once was. Just as digital editing made cutting film a thing of the past, iMovie for iPad does away with the desktop entirely, allowing you to make movies on the move. Drag and drop clips you've shot or imported, add music and titles and share your creations on YouTube in minutes.

See Apps in depth, page 136

Adobe Ideas
Free

If you have an idea that you need to scribble down, don't risk losing it on a scrap of paper or the classic beer mat – use Adobe Ideas. This simple tool offers vector drawing and painting and works with an external display when used with the iPad VGA/HDMI adaptor.

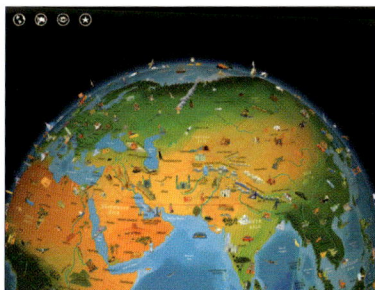

Barefoot World Atlas
£5.49

Based on the book of the same name, this app turns your iPad into an interactive globe you can spin and zoom in on to view animations and text about animals, culture, landmarks and other topics. Aimed at children, it's fascinating for anyone with an interest in geography.

Björk: Biophilia
£8.99

She's known for sonic innovation, but Björk pushed the technology front too with her last album, *Biophilia*. Its iPad app includes 10 mini-apps, one per song, with a mix of interactive art, games and animation. It's creative, playful and pulls you deeper into the music rather than distracting from it.

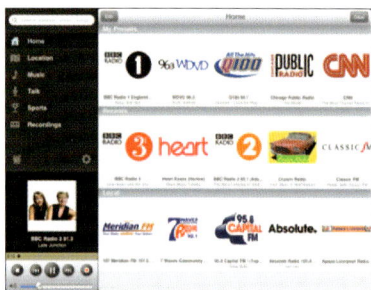

TuneIn Radio Pro
£0.59

Listen to your favourite radio stations from a choice of over 40,000 with TuneIn Radio Pro. Compatible with both iPhone and iPad, this handy little app allows users to record shows, search content and pause live streams for up to half an hour.

Brian Cox's Wonders of the Universe
£4.99

Professor Brian Cox has been opening people's eyes to the wonders of astronomy on TV and in books, but this iPad app combines the best of both. Text from two of his books is joined by photos and video footage in an innovative interface that has no virtual page-turns in sight.

SketchBook Pro
£4.99

Autodesk makes great desktop software and has transitioned beautifully to the iPad with SketchBook Pro. This professional-quality app offers a range of digital art tools including 75 preset brushes with pressure sensitivity, and symmetric drawing.

Twitter
Free

If you're addicted to all things Twitter, the service has a good-looking iPad app that will meet all your 140 character-based needs. The interface is slick, allowing you to swipe between views such as @replies and direct messages. You can set push notifications so you know when you receive new messages too.

See Apps in depth, page 124

BBC iPlayer
Free

iPlayer is a must-have app for iPad, allowing UK licence fee payers to watch BBC shows from the last week on demand. With over 400 hours of programmes to choose from, this will have you glued to your iPad screen.

See Apps in depth, page 146

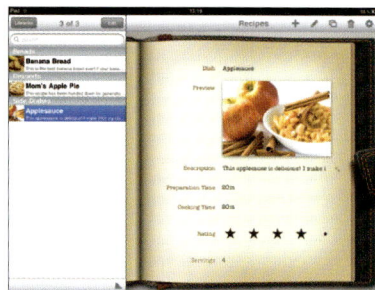

Bento
£2.99

This deliciously designed app is the ultimate tool for organising contacts, planning events, budgeting or just making a to-do list. Perfect when used in conjunction with Bento for Mac or as a standalone product for multiple tasks.

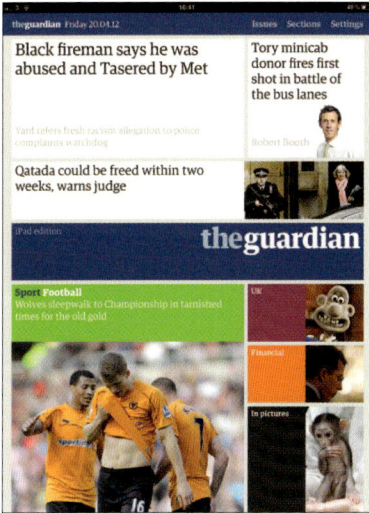

Guardian iPad Edition
£9.99 a month

Many newspaper apps are basically digitised pages from their print editions. *The Guardian*'s more tablet-friendly design offers every story from the newspaper, but includes image galleries, videos and social sharing features, with a slinky swipe-based interface.

iBooks
Free

One of the iPad's many unmissable features, ebook reading is offered in the form of iBooks, which includes a reader and a book store. Download titles like you do apps and they're ready to read. Font size and brightness can be adjusted to your liking and the page turn transition and bookmark features add to the reading experience.

See Start up, page 42

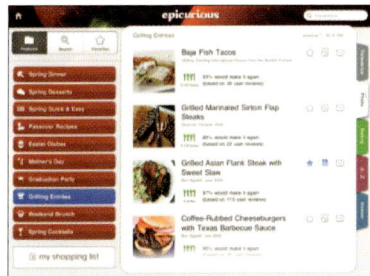

Remote
Free

Take control of your home entertainment with Apple's free Remote App, which gives you wireless control of iTunes and Apple TV from your iPad. Skip songs, select playlists, and browse movies, trailers and YouTube videos on your HD TV.

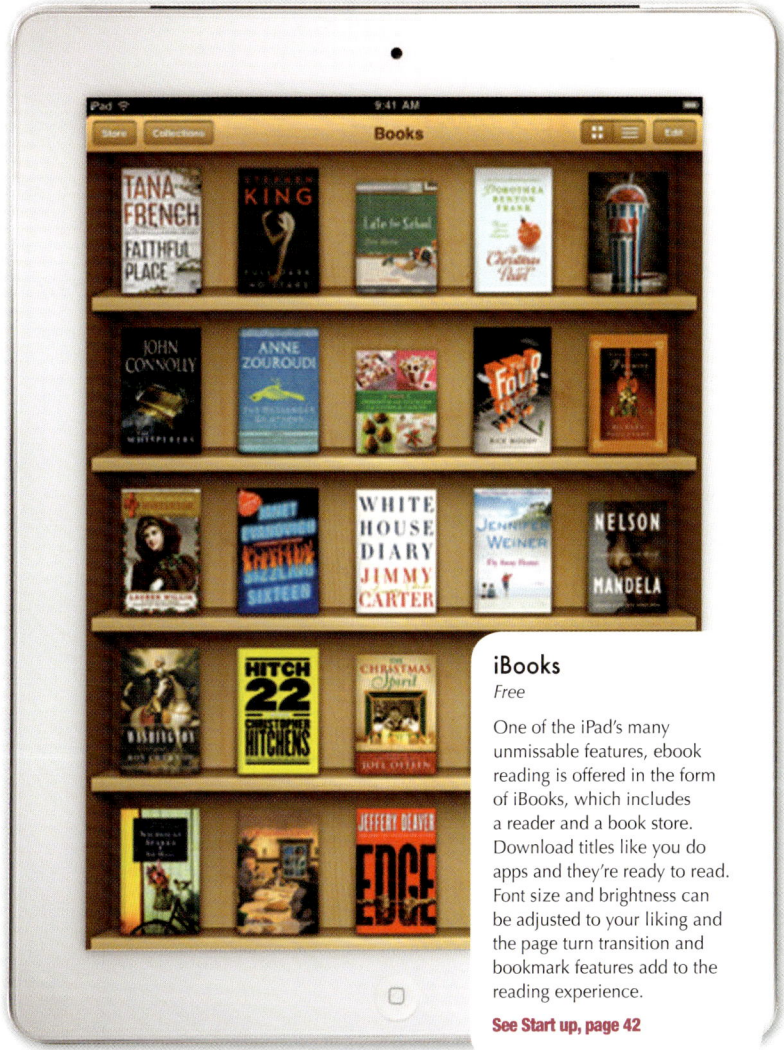

Epicurious Recipes & Shopping List
Free

Stuck for a something to cook? Not sure what to do with the three eggs in your fridge? Epicurious can help. Simply type in your ingredients or search food types to find hundreds of recipes. It'll even make you a shopping list.

Cinderella – Nosy Crow
£5.49

There are some beautiful book-apps for children on the iPad, with Cinderella one of the best-crafted. It tells the fairy tale through animation and interactivity, as kids clean the kitchen, build Cinderella's carriage and choose music for her dance with the prince.

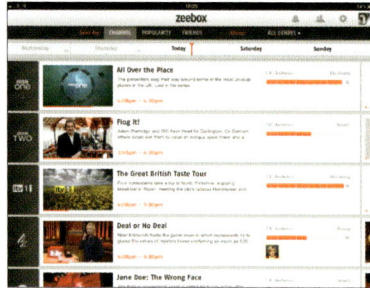

Zeebox
Free

Zeebox is one of a new breed of apps designed for use while you're watching TV. Tell it what you're viewing, and it serves up related tweets, Wikipedia entries, iTunes links and other content. It also works as a social programme guide, letting you know what friends are watching.

djay
£11.99

It was inevitable that the iPad's touchscreen would become a platform for music, and djay is a prime example. Mimicking a complete turntable setup, the app takes in music from your iPod library and allows you to mix tracks and match beats.

Netflix
£5.99 a month

Online TV and films service Netflix streams to a range of devices, including desktop computers, TVs and games consoles. Its iPad app is perfect for catching a movie or two in bed, with an increasing selection of content to choose from.

See Apps in depth, page 146

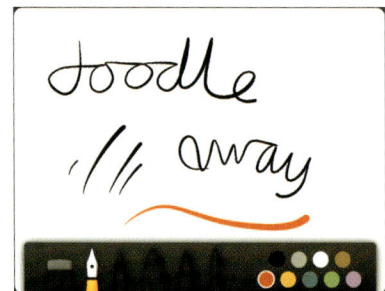

Dropbox
Free

If you already use Dropbox you'll be glad to see it on the iPad. If you're not, you're missing out on a free file sharing service that syncs to your desktop (and now your iPad) so you can access important files from anywhere with an Internet connection. A number of popular iPad apps also include Dropbox integration.

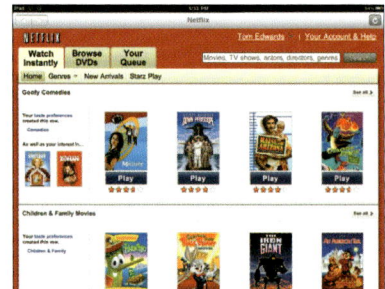

Paper by FiftyThree
Free

Paper says it's all about ideas: helping you draw diagrams, illustrations, sketches and notes. At its best on the new iPad's sharper screen, it makes money by selling you 'tools' at £1.49 a pop, such as a virtual pencil, brush and colours. Ideal for all scribblers.

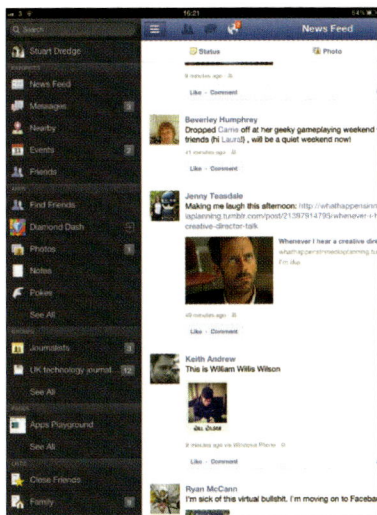

Facebook
Free

Facebook took its time creating a native app for iPad, but the results were well worth it. The app is great for browsing your news feed and posting updates, and particularly impressive when swiping your way through friends' photo albums. A very impressive social dashboard.

See Apps in depth, page 120

IMDb Movies & TV
Free

All the latest movie news, as well as information on that actor who was in that TV show who also starred in the movie you can't remember the name of. You'll use this beautifully crafted movie database app more often than you think.

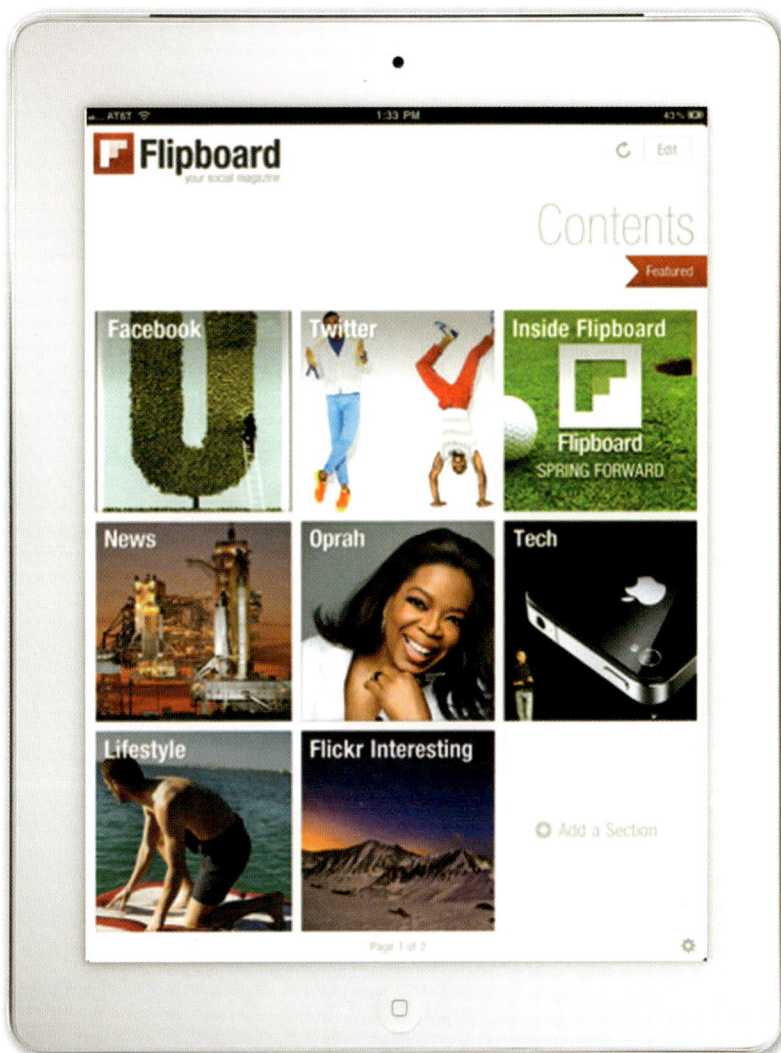

Flipboard
Free

Wouldn't it be nice to see tweets and Facebook updates from people you know and trust presented in a slick magazine format? Well now you can with Flipboard, a clever app that pulls in the feeds from your Twitter and Facebook accounts as well as any others you may wish to add. It's like seeing your friends in print.

Sky Go
Free

BSkyB's iPad app is the perfect way to watch shows if your main TV is tied up or you're away from home. It serves up live streams of Sky's sports, film, lifestyle and news channels, albeit only the ones you have access to at home. It's free, but only for existing Sky subscribers.

Night Stand HD – Alarm Clock
£1.19

If you can't bear to be away from your iPad for five minutes, why not put it next to your bed and use it as an alarm clock? With a number of preset displays, weather and alarm settings it's the perfect app for those who like to wake up next to their favourite gadget.

Dragon Dictation
Free

Take the hassle out of typing reminders into your iPad by talking to it instead. This isn't just voice recording, though – it's dictation. Dragon Dictation does a great job of converting your speech to text with impressively few errors.

iA Writer
£0.59

Simple and understated but ideally suited to the task of writing, iA Writer has to be the best tool for writers on the App Store. It features FocusMode, which only shows the last three lines you've written, and a number of excellent touch-based features that don't clutter the interface but help keep your text as the primary focus.

Kindle
Free

If you're not taken with iBooks or it doesn't have a title you're after, try Amazon's Kindle app as an alternative. Browse books on the Kindle store and buy them from the Amazon site to enjoy on your iPad wherever you may be.

Pages
£5.99

Just like the Mac desktop equivalent, Pages for iPad is a beautifully crafted app with multiple features. It's more than just a word processor, offering page layout functions for a wide range of tasks from projects to posters.

iPhoto
£2.99

Apple's desktop photo-editing software got a tablet revamp in time for the debut of the new iPad, and is a hugely impressive way to sort and edit your collection of photographs. Multi-touch controls and a range of effects spruce up your shots, and a handy Photo Journal feature helps you share the results with friends.

See Apps in depth, page 132

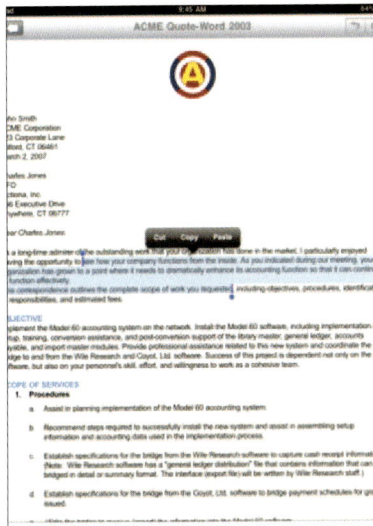

Documents To Go – Office Suite
£5.99

An office suite for your iPad, Documents To Go adds compatibility with a number of non-iPad file formats and lets you edit them too. A desktop app allows you to sync your documents wirelessly.

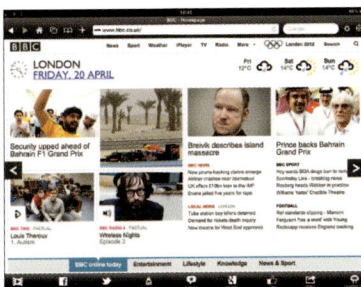

Skyfire Web Browser for iPad
£2.99

The iPad famously doesn't play nice with Adobe's Flash technology, which is bad news for websites that use it. Skyfire lets you watch Flash videos, and includes a HotSwap mode that lets different users browse with their own bookmarks and settings.

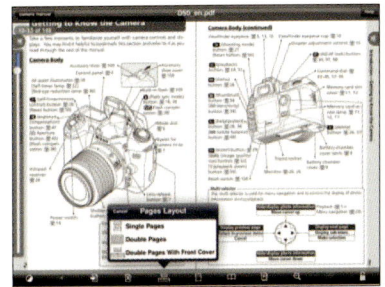

GoodReader for iPad
£2.99

Open your iPad to more formats than it's used to and access giant PDF and .txt files with GoodReader. Annotate documents, sync files and transfer them regardless of their size or content.

Skype for iPad
Free

Skype is one of the best Voice-over-IP apps for cheap calls to friends and family, but that's only part of the appeal of its iPad app. Full-screen video calls make it a viable alternative to Apple's FaceTime, especially as it can talk to non-Apple devices.

SlingPlayer Mobile for iPad
£17.99

If you have a Slingbox you'll know how easy it is to watch your home TV on any computer. The SlingPlayer app adds this TV viewing functionality to your iPad, so you don't miss your favourite shows, even when you're abroad.

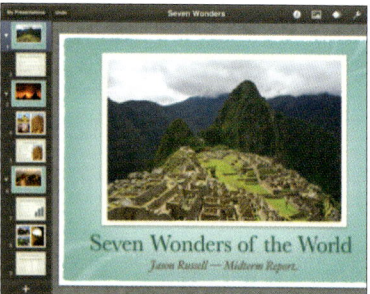

BBC News
Free

The best news stories and a 24-hour live feed of news are all available in this well-crafted app from the BBC. Customise the interface to suit your news preferences and hit the 'Live' button to get updates on the latest goings-on, wherever you are. An essential app for use with your morning coffee.

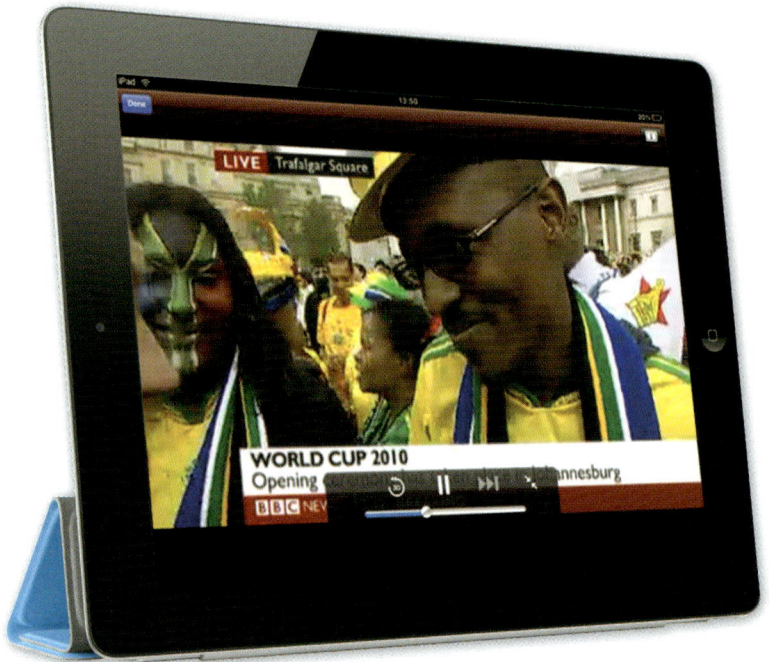

Keynote
£5.99

Building engaging presentations has long been the sole territory of Microsoft PowerPoint – but not any more. Apple's answer is Keynote: the iPad version offers a wide range of themes and transitions, helping you create professional, dynamic slideshows wherever you are.

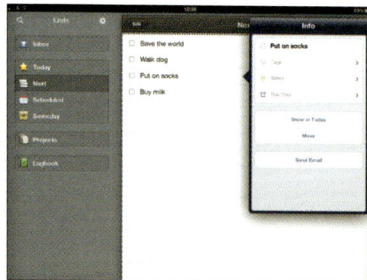

Things for iPad
£13.99

Lots of personal organiser apps are available for the iPad, but Things remains one of the easiest to use, while also providing plenty of features. At its most basic it's a To-Do list app, but it can handle bigger projects too. If you own the separate Mac version, it syncs wirelessly with that too.

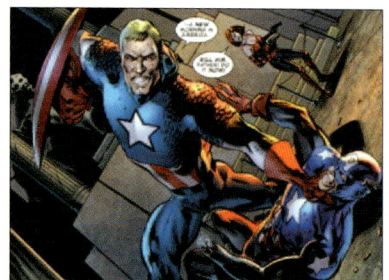

Comics
Free

If you never grew out of the joys of immersing yourself in a good comic, this app's for you. Comics for iPad brings you comics from the very best publishers, including Marvel and DC, while the new iPad's lush Retina display means reading them is still a magical experience.

Magic Piano
£0.59

Not exactly a professional music tool but still a lot of fun, Magic Piano offers a unique way to play popular songs by following lights on the screen. There are also two other keyboard displays for more casual play.

Toca Kitchen
£1.49

Far less messy and dangerous than letting your children cook real food, Toca Kitchen is a marvellously fun app that gets them slicing, dicing, frying and boiling virtual fruit, veg'n'meat for four cartoon characters, who show their appreciation. Playful, but educational too.

Vevo HD for iPad
Free

Online, Vevo wants to be the Web 2.0 generation's MTV, serving up more than 45,000 music videos. Its iPad app is slick and perfect for bitesize viewing, complete with Facebook and Twitter sharing features, and the option to wirelessly stream to AirPlay-compatible TVs or the Apple TV set-top box.

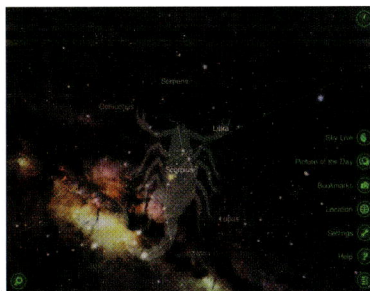

WildChords
Free

Children learning to play the guitar aren't stuck with stern-faced music teachers any more. WildChords is an iPad app that teaches chords, melodies and scales within a game format, using the microphone to recognise when you're playing the right notes. Initially free, extra lessons cost 69p a time.

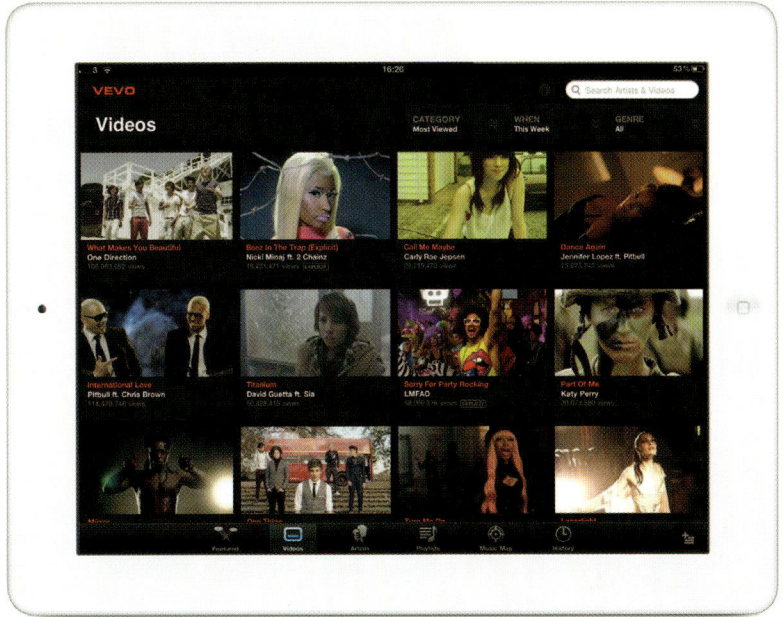

Star Walk for iPad
£2.99

Much of the hype around augmented reality technology is overblown, but Star Walk is one of the examples that makes jaws drop. Point your iPad at the night sky, and the app tells you what all the stars, constellations and satellites are, throwing in a calendar to suggest the best times to look.

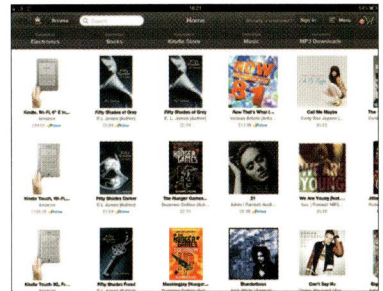

Amazon Windowshop
Free

Amazon's website works well enough in the iPad's browser, but the company's Windowshop app makes everything a bit, well... whizzier. It's based around product images and swiping controls, making it easy and intuitive to browse and buy items from the online store. Perfect for sofa-shopping sessions.

The 50 iPad games you have to play

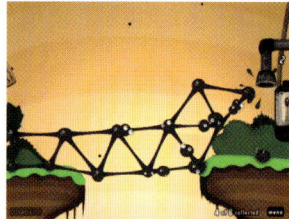

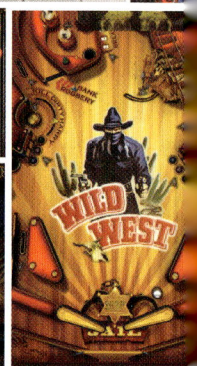

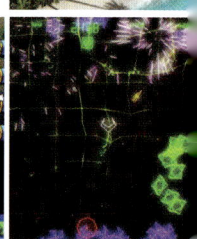

From fiendishly addictive puzzlers to fast, furious shoot 'em ups, the App Store offers something for everyone…

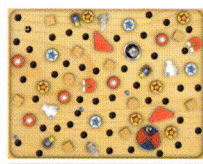

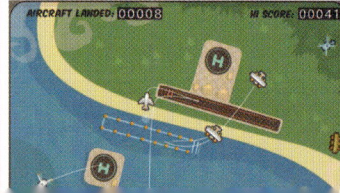

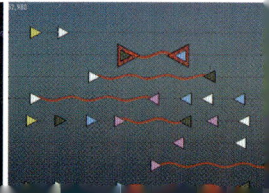

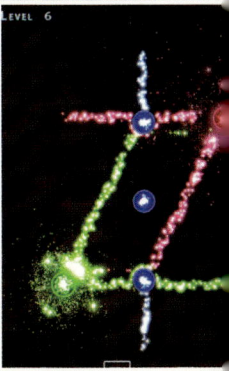

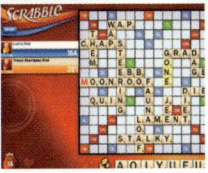

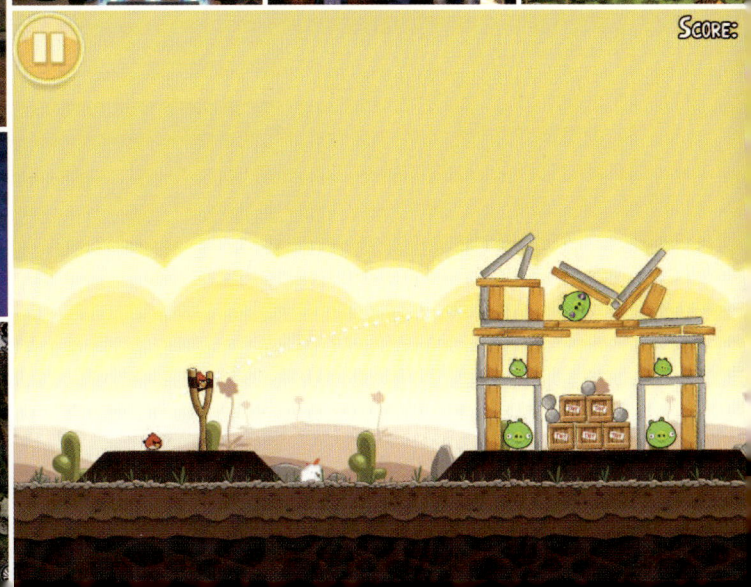

Tetris for iPad
£4.99

People are playing Tetris on their iPads in 2012? Yes, even though it's quite expensive. What you get are several modes, a one-touch control option that's well suited to the touchscreen, and a slightly clunky in-app purchases system. But the core block-dropping gameplay makes amends for all flaws, and then some.

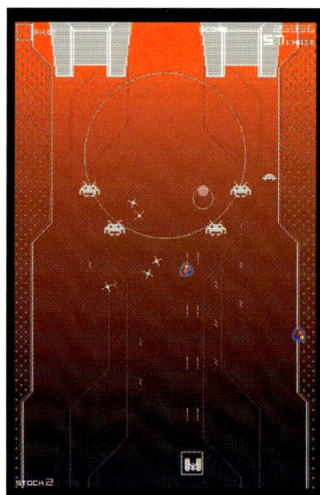

Cut the Rope HD
£1.19

Chillingo's delightful little time-waster is rapidly approaching Angry Birds-esque levels of ubiquity, and with good reason. Its ingenious gameplay, in which you attempt to feed a lizard-like creature candy by snipping the rope from which it hangs, is thoroughly moreish. Easy to play but hard to master, this is a cute, content-heavy gem.

Civilization Revolution for iPad
£7.49

The hugely popular PC strategy series survives being shrunk down for the iPad, offering a fun, accessible war sim. There's not quite as much going on as the franchise faithful might be accustomed to, but there's still plenty here for your money.

Space Invaders Infinity Gene
£2.99

Arcade veteran Taito completely reinvents its decades-old classic, creating a bonkers, brilliant shooter that piles on mad idea after mad idea. One of the very best top-down shooters you'll play on any system, with enough content to keep you playing for hours.

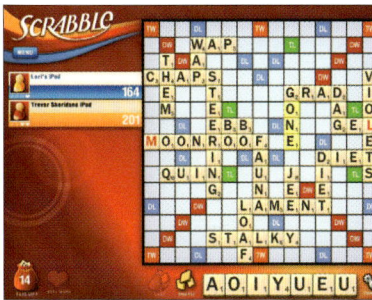

Scrabble for iPad
£3.99

It's Scrabble. On your iPad. What more do you want? Any lingering doubts you might have had about whether Apple's device was worth the cash will be dispelled once you've enjoyed a long-haul flight with this slick conversion of the perennial board game favourite for company.

Contre Jour HD
£1.99

If there's an equivalent in iPad gaming to artsy indie movies, Contre Jour HD might well be it. You play a little critter called Petit, who you have to guide through a succession of eerily bewitching levels by pulling, pushing and tapping the scenery and objects around him.

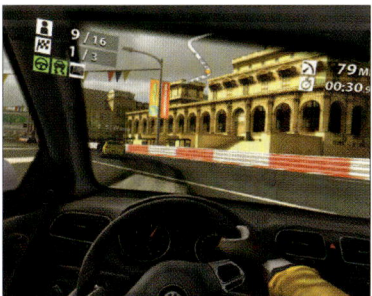

Real Racing 2 HD
£5.99

Of all the tilt-to-turn racers vying for pole position on the App Store grid, this is the slickest, speediest and most feature-heavy. The £5.99 price tag might seem steep, but that gets you both a 10-hour campaign and local or online multiplayer over 15 different tracks.

Plants vs. Zombies HD
£3.99

From the same genius factory that brought you the fiendishly addictive timesinks Bejeweled and Peggle, Plants vs. Zombies HD should be your first port of call when you unwrap your new iPad. The bonkers concept sees you defending your home from wave after wave of zombie invaders by planting various projectile-lobbing strains of flora. Beautifully presented and furiously addictive, this is portable joy.

Mass Effect Infiltrator
£2.99

EA really hit its stride with hardcore games for iPad in the last year or so, and Mass Effect Infiltrator is an excellent spin-off from the popular console series. It involves yomping around a space base shooting robots and mutants, while admiring some genuinely eye-boggling graphics.

Speedball 2 Evolution
£1.79

One for the veteran gamers, Speedball 2 Evolution is a classy update of the Amiga classic, complete with WiFi multiplayer and handsome new HD visuals. For the uninitiated, imagine a futuristic cocktail of football, hockey and bar-room brawling.

Labyrinth 2 HD
£4.99

The classic tilt-and-roll marble maze game gets a smart iPad update, boasting a barrel-load of new stages as well as access to thousands of user-created efforts. There's four-way multiplayer, new maze elements and achievements to rack up.

Zombie Infection HD
£2.99

The same crew behind N.O.V.A. 2 and Dungeon Hunter attempt to re-skin the hugely successful Resident Evil franchise for the iPad and with some success. As guilty pleasures go, nonchalantly head-shooting a brain-hungry denizen of the undead is tough to beat.

World of Goo HD
£2.99

It might not get as much press as the likes of Angry Birds or Cut the Rope, but ask a dedicated gamer what the finest title in the App Store is and there's a good chance they'll bring up this wonderful creation. Your task is to stretch balls of sentient goo into precarious structures to provide access to an escape pipe. Eccentric, charming and very challenging.

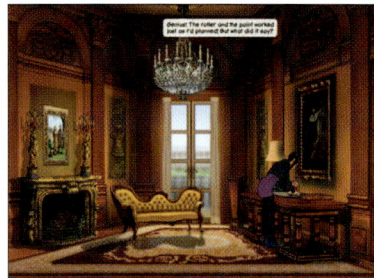

Broken Sword: Director's Cut HD
£3.49

Looking for a meatier experience than the average pick-up-and-play title? This is it: a lavish HD makeover of the '90s PC adventure game. The point-and-click exploration works well and the twisty plot is a match for any airport thriller.

Crimson: Steam Pirates
Free

Bungie made its name with Halo on console, but the firm is trying on a new hat, publishing indie developers' iOS games. Crimson: Steam Pirates was the first, and is an excellent slice of turn-based strategy action, with a piratical theme. You get one chapter for free, then pay for further ones.

Tiny Tower
Free

A 'freemium' building game, but one that provides a great contrast to Zynga's CityVille, since you're building a single tower and packing it with businesses and residents. The pixel-art graphics have bags of character, none of which is lost when blown up to iPad-size.

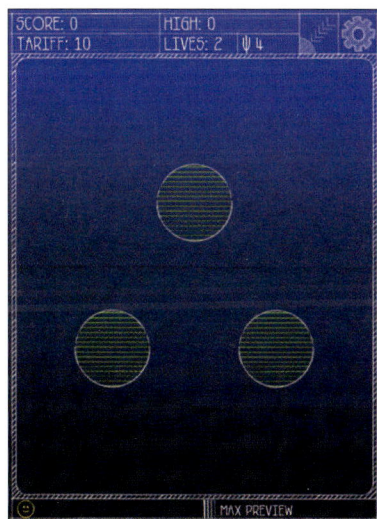

Minecraft: Pocket Edition
£4.99

Mojang's indie PC hit has made the transition to iPad with aplomb, as you explore a blocky world and build whatever you like. You can invite friends in for the fun with its local multiplayer mode too. It's digital Lego for grown-ups, and wonderfully creative with it too.

Magnetic Billiards: Blueprint
Free

Imagine playing pool if there were no pockets, and balls could only be removed if you stuck them together in clusters. That's Magnetic Billiards: Blueprint, which is one of the most addictive games available for iPad. There's plenty of fun to be had for free, but extra modes and tables can be bought in-game.

BIT.TRIP BEAT HD
£0.59

Essentially Pong on industrial-strength hallucinogens, BIT.TRIP BEAT HD is an insane little thing. It's brutally hard, but so eye-poppingly out-there that you'll gladly come back for a second thrashing. What's more, its chip-tune soundtrack is ear candy of the highest order.

Flight Control Rocket
£0.69

The original Flight Control was a huge hit on iPad and iPhone alike, as you guided aeroplanes in to land. Its sequel shifts the action to Space, with 15 spacecraft to land, and pin-sharp colourful visuals that show off the new iPad's Retina screen at its best.

Grand Theft Auto 3
£2.99

It's 10 years since Grand Theft Auto 3 came out on consoles, but its gameplay still feels fresh and innovative on the iPad in 2012. The characters, missions and Liberty City setting remain the same, but the controls have been reworked for the touchscreen to great effect.

Sid Meier's Pirates! for iPad
£2.99

Originally a hit on C64 and Amiga computers, before a later revival on Xbox 360, this piratical adventure remains just as good on a touchscreen. Sail the Caribbean battling ships, sacking cities, romancing governors' daughters and capturing famous pirates. Rollicking fun.

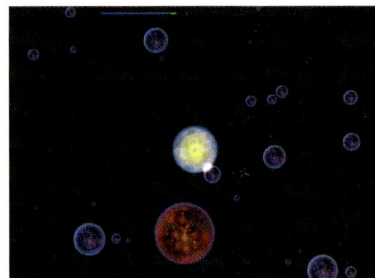

Osmos for iPad
£2.99

An impossible-to-pigeonhole title that sees you trying to grow a floating blob by delicately prodding it around the screen to absorb other, smaller blobs. It's a unique, ambient, zen-like plaything – just the thing after a day fighting your way through the rat race.

Super Stickman Golf
£0.59

Ignore the title – this delightful game has very little to do with the pensioner's game of choice. Instead, it's a crafty physics-based platformer that sees you attempting to ping your ball through a series of fiendish stages with the help of a variety of over-the-top power-ups. Highly recommended.

Angry Birds Space HD
£1.99

The latest Angry Birds game shakes up the feather-flinging formula subtly, yet effectively. You're still hurling furious birds at egg-stealing pigs, but this time it's in Space, with planets and gravitational fields to cope with. Casual players will have plenty of fun, but hardcore types will obsess on completing levels with three-star ratings.

SCORE
0

HIGHSCORE
89570

Galaxy On Fire 2
£5.99

Anyone old enough to remember space trading classic Elite? If you still miss that game, this should be right up your street. It's an enormous intergalactic adventure of the scale you'd expect to find on your PC, not a humble tablet. Invest the time and there are months' worth of missions to get stuck into here.

The Settlers HD
£0.59

Arguably the most successful attempt at squeezing a full PC real-time strategy experience into the confines of the iPad, The Settlers HD is crammed with content and just about manages to eke out a sensible control system from the touchscreen. Some knowledge of the genre is necessary, though.

Reckless Racing HD
£2.99

If Real Racing 2 is the iPad's answer to Gran Turismo, Reckless Racing is surely its Mario Kart. It's a madcap top-down racer that sees you hooning around eight different tracks at breakneck speed, complete with online multiplayer and leaderboards for the competitively spirited.

Puzzle Quest 2
£2.99

Essentially a classy Bejeweled clone with a side order of immersive RPG trimmings, this is just the thing for iPad gamers who like to mix in a little Dungeons & Dragons with their casual match-three puzzling. At £2.99, there's plenty of game for your money too.

Fibble HD
£2.99

Fibble HD's makers have some hardcore gaming credentials – they created PC games Far Cry and Crysis. Their first iPad game is more accessible: a physics puzzler that sees you rolling an alien called Fibble around an Earthling's house as he gathers friends to fly home.

Brothers In Arms 2: Global Front HD
£0.59

A sturdy, scaled-down version of the popular console and PC shooter, this won't win awards for originality but it delivers solid thrills. The virtual D-pad controls are as tricksy as ever, but persevere and there's plenty of bang for your buck here.

Dead Space for iPad
£5.99

Further proof, should any be needed, that the iPad can handle 'proper' games. Rather than rushing out a cheap, clumsy port of its bestselling console survival horror series, EA has produced a standalone game. Not only does it look fantastic and nail the touchscreen controls in a way that few action games really have, it's ruddy terrifying too. You have been warned.

Draw Something
Free / £0.69

With 50m downloads and counting, Draw Something is a craze – and one at its best on the iPad's larger screen. It's like a Facebook-fuelled Pictionary, as you draw pictures of words for friends to guess, and vice versa. It's turn-based, so you don't have to be online at the same time – and you can have several games going at once.

Superbrothers: Sword & Sworcery EP
£2.99

The latest effort from the team that brought you delightful iPhone puzzler Critter Crunch is a weird and wonderful adventure game that puts an artsy 21st-century twist on Nintendo's beloved Zelda template. It's an absolutely bewitching experience, really pushing the boundaries of what an iPad game can achieve, both sonically and visually. An essential purchase.

LEGO Harry Potter: Years 1-4
£1.79

A fantastic debut for the LEGO series proper in the App Store, and a must for fans of the boy wizard. If you've played the LEGO games on other systems you'll know what to expect: tongue-in-cheek adventuring, moreish collectible hunting and character customisation options aplenty.

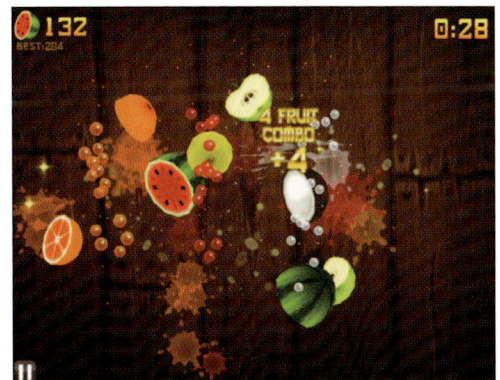

Fruit Ninja HD
£1.79

The game's basic concept – chop up fruit by swiping across the screen – is so absurdly simple that you wonder how it could possibly sustain a compelling game. But boy, does it ever. There's something supremely satisfying about dicing a watermelon to ribbons with a samurai sword.

N.O.V.A. 2 – Near Orbit Vanguard Alliance HD
£3.99

Pegging itself as the iPad's answer to best-selling Xbox shooter Halo, N.O.V.A. offers some very sturdy, albeit supremely generic, space marine-centric blasting thrills. The basic single-player campaign is a boisterous thrill-ride – but the real fun comes in the online multiplayer modes, which see you competing for bragging rights with up to nine other players.

Football Manager Handheld 2012
£6.99

The latest incarnation of Sports Interactive and Sega's football manager game runs like a dream on the iPad, with its gripping blend of tactics, transfers and training intact, along with new features like a Challenge mode and Apple TV support to play on an even bigger screen.

RAGE HD
£1.19

From the same people that brought us shoot 'em up classics Doom and Quake, RAGE HD is a gruesome shooting gallery released to tie-in with the forthcoming PC and console title of the same name. It's not for the faint-hearted, but this is as good as the genre gets on the App Store.

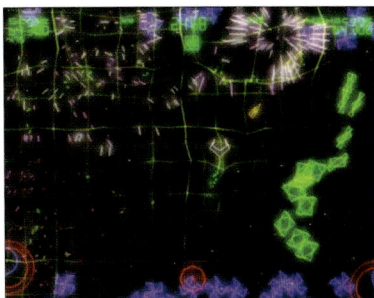

Geometry Wars: Touch
£0.59

Purists will argue that this iOS take on the hugely popular Xbox 360 blaster suffers without actual thumbsticks – but stick with it and there's masses of fun to be had here. Think arcade classic Asteroids turned all the way up to 11 – this is a fast and furious assault on the senses.

Boggle for iPad
£1.79

Another handy weapon in the fight against long-haul flight boredom. The iPad is the perfect fit for the classic word game and developer EA hasn't skimped on the features, offering every imaginable game mode and a multiplayer permutation. A no-brainer.

Chopper 2
£1.79

Remember playing Choplifter on the Commodore 64? Whoever made this fun little action game certainly does. You control the titular aircraft by tilting your iPad from left to right, zooming around stages in search of hostages to airlift to safety or enemy bases to destroy.

Mirror's Edge
£2.99

Another twist on the Canabalt template, this impressive effort really stands on its own two feet. You have to guide your rogue free-runner across rooftops and through enemy facilities, dodging obstacles by swiping across the touchscreen to perform a variety of different jumps and slides. It's hugely satisfying once you master the controls and lock into a smooth flow.

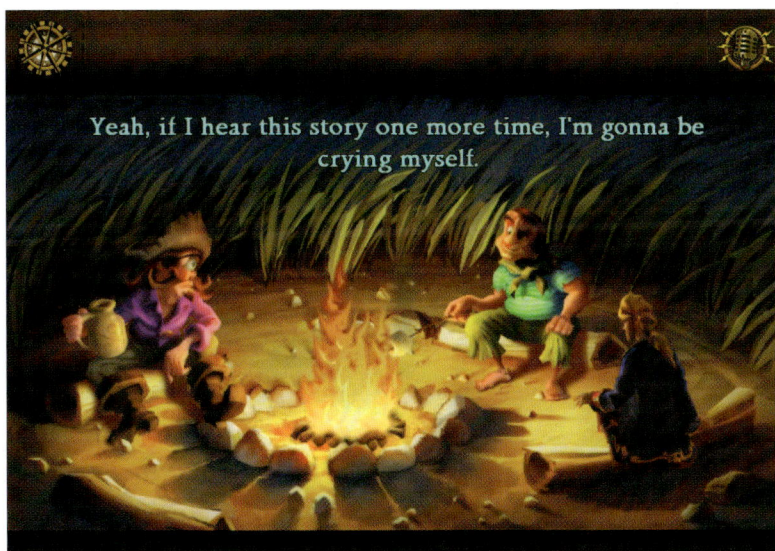

Secret of Monkey Island: Special Edition, for iPad
£2.99

This lovingly crafted HD remake of the classic '90s PC adventure proves that not everything diminishes with age. It's still a hugely enjoyable romp, not to mention certifiably insane, and has never looked better. A delightful trip down memory lane and a great game in its own right.

Order & Chaos Online
£4.99

Gameloft's massively multiplayer RPG wants to be iPad's answer to World of Warcraft. You choose from four races and adventure through a sprawling world completing quests, slaying monsters and interacting with other players. It's genuinely absorbing stuff.

Whale Trail
£0.69

Another game, like Draw Something, that's also available on iPhone but really benefits from the iPad's big screen. Whale Trail has you swooping through the clouds as Willow the Whale, collecting bubbles. It's psychedelic, wonderfully-crafted and addictive as hell.

Infinity Blade II
£4.99

Another sequel to an iOS hit here, as Infinity Blade returns with even better-looking hacking, slashing and… well, more hacking and slashing. You battle against a succession of enormous monsters with swipes and taps, with innovative 'ClashMob' social features connecting you with friends as you go.

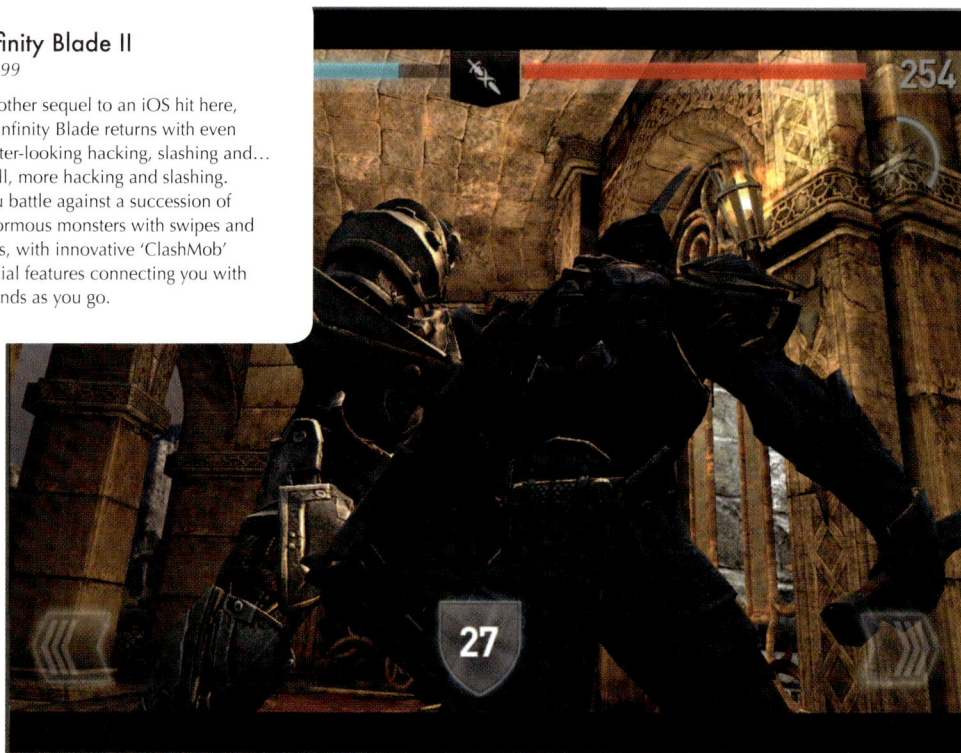

Sky Gamblers: Air Supremacy
£2.99

If you're looking to show off the new iPad's Retina display and beefy processor, Sky Gamblers is the game to do it with. An air combat game, its visuals are stunning as you swoop through cityscapes dogfighting with other planes. Online multiplayer modes add depth once you complete the solo challenges.

My Horse
Free

Owning a horse in the real world is pricey, but owning a virtual one on your iPad is free. Well, unless you start going mad with in-app purchases to primp your ride. The game sees you grooming and feeding your horse, before entering it in contests. Graphics and animation are sumptuous, too.

CityVille Hometown
Free

Zynga's CityVille game is hugely popular on Facebook, and this standalone spin-off is just as entertaining on iPad. The pitch: SimCity with a social twist, as you build a town, connect to friends and make lots of virtual money.

Get to grips with GarageBand on the iPad

▶ GarageBand on the Mac has long been an impressive tool for musicians. Sure, it's not Pro Tools, but then Pro Tools costs a fortune, whereas GarageBand comes free on all Macs. Now, this multi-track recorder and music simulation app is available on the iPad, and the power beneath its touchscreen interface is frankly amazing.

For just £2.99, Apple has crammed in an incredible array of music tools: Smart Instruments almost play themselves, virtual instruments put all kinds of sounds at your fingertips, and a full eight-track recorder lets you construct your songs. You can even hook up with your mates on other iOS devices and jam together – and needless to say, it works with iCloud to boot. Here's our walkthrough that'll have you composing like a maestro, pronto.

VITAL INFO

In our detailed guide, we'll show you how to compose a belting tune from scratch, record from real world and Smart instruments, and share your tracks with the world at large.

What you need
New iPad
GarageBand app (£2.99)
Guitar and guitar cable (optional)

Time required
How long have you got?

Flip reverse

Use these buttons to flip between multi-track view and the instrument view.

Play/Record

Your stop, play and record controls are here. A selected track (highlighted in green) will be recorded on when you hit the red button.

Instrumental

Tap 'Instruments' to select from an array of instruments to record with on your track.

Add sounds

Add a track using the '+' button at the base of the track selector pane on the left of the screen. Hide the track options by swiping the tab on the right of the column.

Multi-tracking

The right-hand pane shows a timeline of all the tracks (up to a standard eight) on your tune. Don't worry, it's easier to use than it looks!

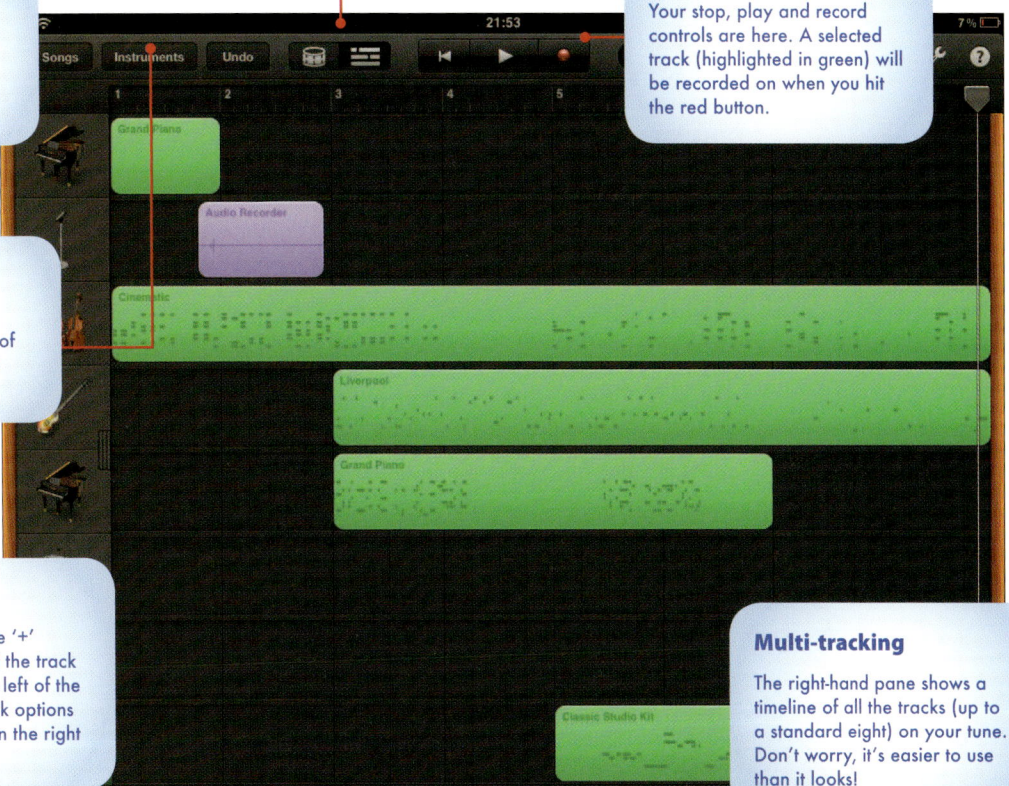

Play a tune

Switch to instrument view and you'll see this screen. We've selected the microphone here, but each instrument has its own unique interface – we'll explain, fear not.

NEED TO KNOW
A little help

The '?' icon in the top right-hand corner of the screen is your safety net. Tap it at any time, and up pop helpful bubbles explaining all the options on screen. Another tap toggles it off again.

Step-by-step guide ▶▶▶

Learn to play Smart Instruments

Apple touts Smart Instruments as a tool that lets anyone make music, regardless of their musical talent – or lack thereof. Essentially, they're automated instruments that allow you to compose music by picking out chords, or in the case of drums, by selecting how you want your beat to be constructed. Here's how they work…

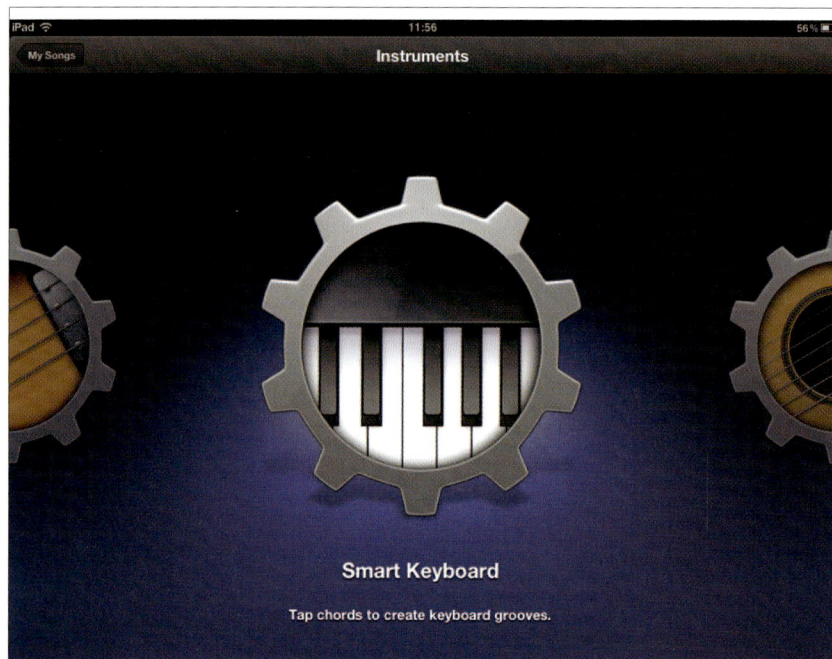

Smart Keyboard

Tap chords to create keyboard grooves.

1 From the main screen, tap 'Instruments' and swipe across to find the Smart Instrument you want to play – they all have a cog symbol around them. We're going to start with the Smart Keyboard – so give that one a tap.

2 Every one of the Smart Instruments has its own unique look and feel: even different kinds of keyboard look distinct from one another. Tap the 'Grand Piano' icon to see what other kinds of keyboard there are to choose from. Pick one to see – and hear – the difference.

3 We've picked the Electric Piano. Set 'Autoplay' to 'Off' to play the notes in each chord displayed and learn as you go. Alternatively, switch Autoplay on – the keyboard will play a different arrangement of each chord on each of the settings, '1' to '4'. The higher you go, the more elaborate it becomes.

**NEED TO KNOW
Different UI**

Each Smart Instrument's interface is slightly different, but look for the similarities. You'll often see a dial for Auto-play on screen, and any image of an instrument probably means that you can select a different type. Lastly, the spanner icon in the top right always lets you change the key, and thus the available chords.

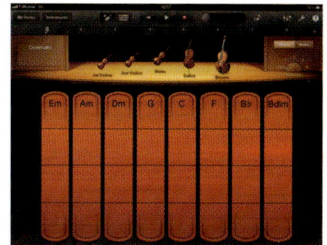

4 On the Electric Piano interface, the top bar of each chord represents the treble and middle notes, while the bottom bar represents the bass note. If you tap the button at the top (the bit that contains the chord name) the whole chord will light up and play.

5 Here's the Hard Rock option from the Smart Guitar instrument. The interfaces for the Smart Guitar and Smart Bass work along much the same lines as the Smart Keyboards, except you don't get the option isolate the bass notes from the rest of the chord.

6 A recent addition to GarageBand is the Smart Strings orchestra. You can conduct a whole pit in much the same way, but as well as picking the different types of sound (cinematic, pop) you can toggle individual instruments on or off to isolate the sounds you want.

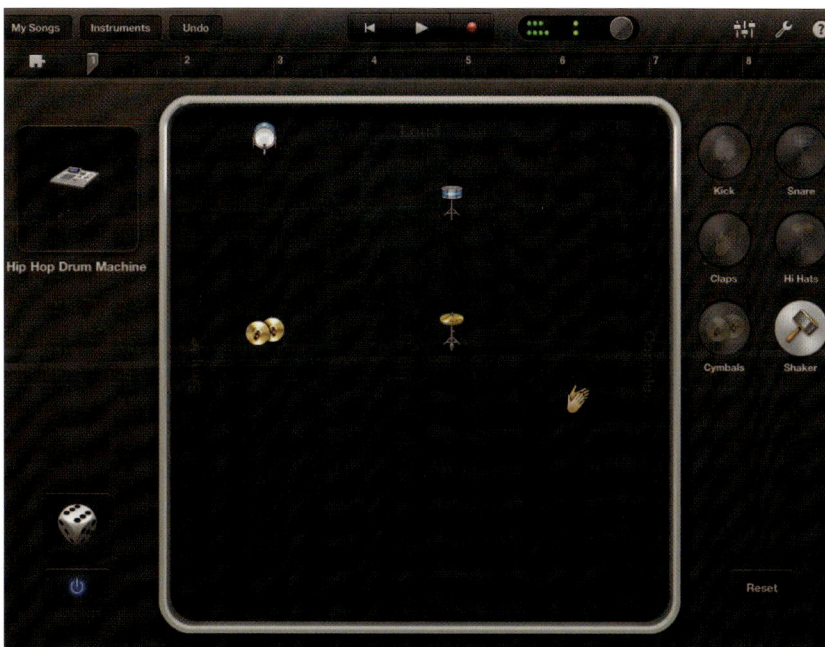

7 Smart Drums work in an entirely different way from the rest of GarageBand's Smart Instruments. Place the drum items on the grid according to the way you want them to sound – the scale goes from 'Simple' to 'Complex' left to right, and from 'Quiet' to 'Loud' bottom to top. Press the die for a random beat.

NEED TO KNOW
Going solo
Smart Keyboards, Strings, Guitar and Bass allow you to choose between 'Chords' and 'Notes' with a switch. Switch to notes, and the stabilizers come off: you can play the instrument yourself – but you'll need to know what you're doing!

Playing the virtual instruments

GarageBand also offers a less automated way of playing music. It's a great way to put your own stamp on your recordings, but it's somewhat harder to master. Here's how to play GarageBand's virtual instruments…

1 From the Instruments screen, pick the Keyboard. Choose a type from the row of categories along the top of the pop-up menu, but keep an eye out as some sub-categories have more than one page. We've chosen 'Supergroup Lead' under 'Synth Leads'.

2 You'll find more options along the right-hand side above the keys, including an option to squeeze two decks on screen. The central 'Scroll' button controls what happens as you slide left and right across the keys – you can add audio effects such as pitch-bending.

3 Now we've switched to the Drums instrument. As you can see, this presents you with a full drum kit to play around with. Press the central button to choose what kind of kit you'd like to play. A 'Live' kit looks like this.

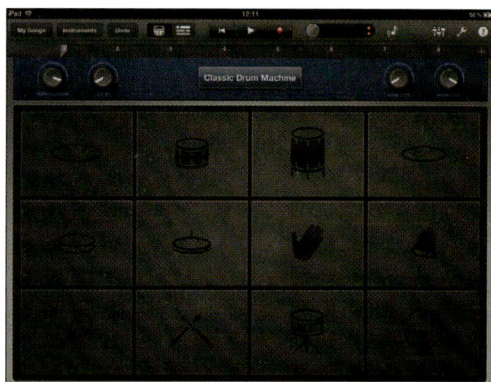

4 Switch to a drum machine kit, and you'll see a grid of pads instead. It's easiest to create a short beat and then loop it in the tracks view. We'll explain this in the 'Create a song in GarageBand' section shortly.

WANT MORE? *EasyBeats 2 Pro Drum Machine (£1.49)*
EasyBeats is a great app for laying down drumbeats. It allows you to create loops and send them as high-quality .wav files to your computer over WiFi.

Recording real instruments and vocals

The new iPad is surprisingly well equipped to record external sounds. The built-in mic is fine for quick demos, while the 3.5mm headphone jack doubles as an input if you use an appropriate third-party gadget such as the guitar input from Griffin we'll be using here, as we look at the guitar amps and how to record.

1 Select 'Guitar Amp' from the Instruments screen. Connect your guitar, pick an amp, and tap the plug icon at the top left. Turn 'Monitor' on to hear your guitar through your headphones. All the dials on the amps are moveable, so you can fine-tune your sound.

2 Tap the icon at the top right that resembles a pedal to set up your effects. You'll see a basic pedal set-up. Tap the empty space to the right of it to see an array of effects, and create your ultimate pedal board.

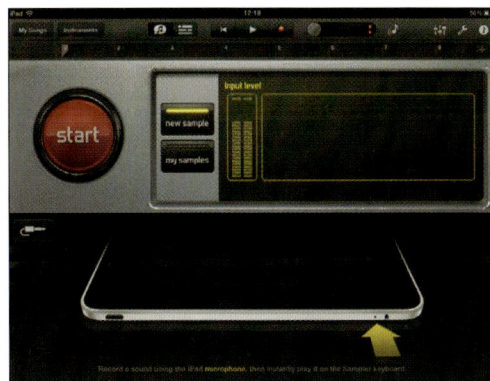

3 Now that your guitar is ready, you can try out the 'Sampler' option from the instrument carousel. This allows you to record a sound using the new iPad's microphone. Tap 'Start' to record a sound, then tap 'Stop'.

4 Your sample will then be mapped to a keyboard, enabling you to play it at different pitches. Depending on what kind of sound you've sampled, you can get some very strange and cool effects using this tool.

NEED TO KNOW
Simple samples
On the sampler, you can tap 'My Samples' to see the sounds you've recorded, as well as a library of stock samples such as dogs barking, laughter, and an "Oh!" sound, to give your track that trashy Europop vibe. Alternatively, try the Audio Recorder from the instruments screen to record your own vocals and add effects to them.

Create a song in GarageBand

GarageBand's instruments tools are impressive, but the real fun starts when you begin to put them together to make a song. We'll approach this as though we've already written the bones of a song and we want to use GarageBand to record and develop it.

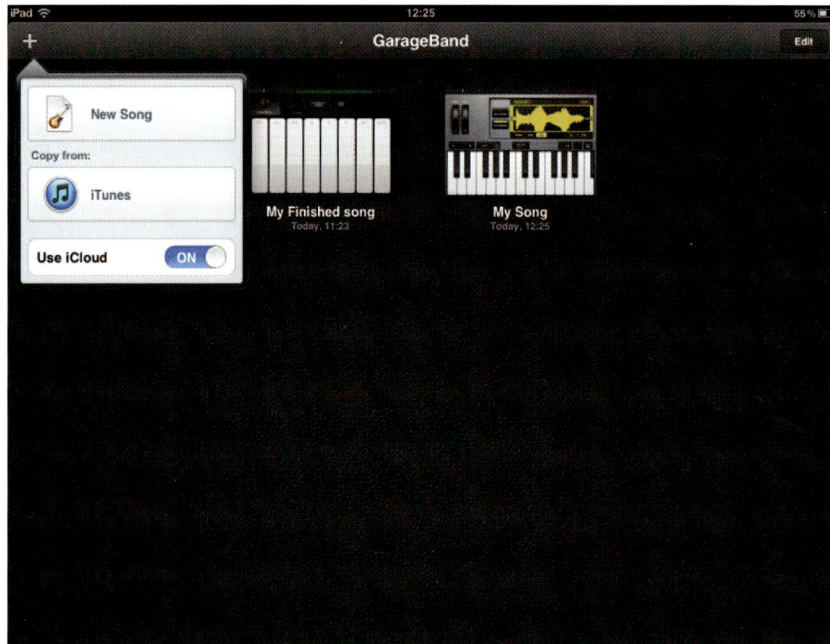

**NEED TO KNOW
Auto Sections**
Sections are great for structuring your composition, but if your song isn't quite ready yet, you can set the section length to 'Automatic'. This allows the section to last as long as you want – great for quickly laying down ideas.

1 Tap 'My Songs' (top-left) to start a new song. Press the '+' sign at the bottom. You can choose to create a new song or duplicate an existing song – useful for working on an alternative mix or version of one of your songs.

2 Pick your first instrument: we've gone for Smart Drums. Before you start playing, tap the '+' icon (top-right) and select how many bars you want the first section (say, the intro) to be.

3 Next, pick a tempo for your song. Tap the spanner icon (top right) and toggle to your preferred tempo. You can also set the metronome to 'on' or 'off' here, and choose a key to play in.

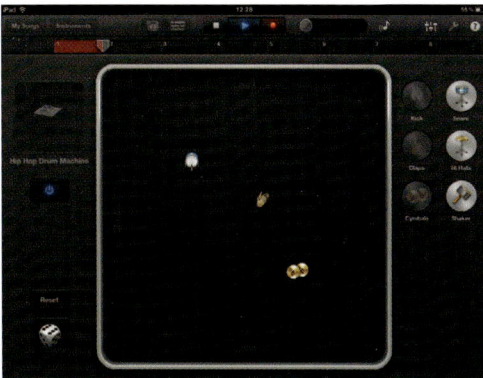

4 Set up the drum beat you want, and when you're ready, press the 'Record' button. The beat will play for the duration of your song section. You can see your recording progress as the bar across the top goes red.

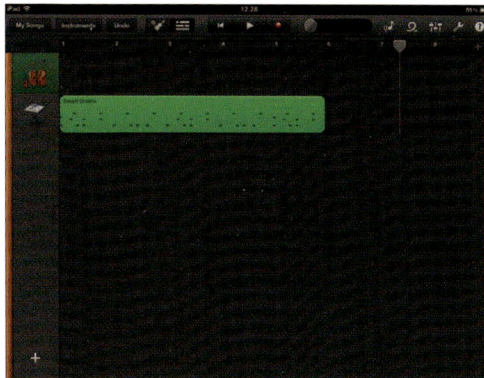

5 Now tap the toggle view button at the top of the screen (directly to the left of the play/record buttons). You can now see your recorded intro on the timeline. Press 'Play' to listen back to it.

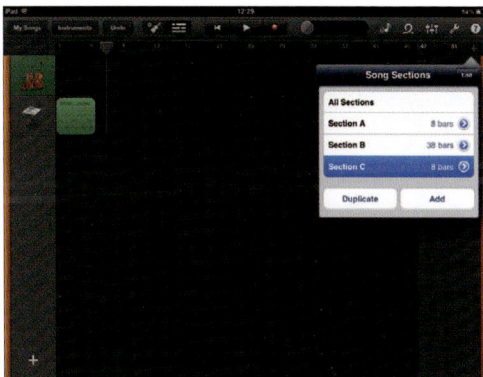

6 Time to add another section. Press the '+' icon again, and press 'Add'. We've created the whole song here in sections, as we already know how it's structured. You can have up to 10 sections.

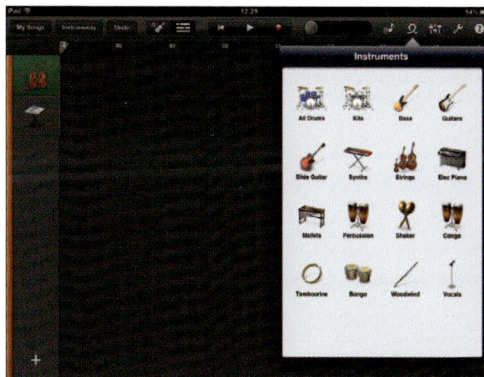

7 At the top-right of the tracks view is yet another option: the loop browser. This lets you preview hundreds of Apple loops – everything from drums to vocals – and add them to your piece.

Continued on next page ❱❱❱

8 We've now structured the drums for our whole song. You can copy and paste bits of recording by tapping segments of a track twice. This brings up a menu. Place the timeline marker where you want your clipping to start and tap ahead of it. A 'Paste' option will appear.

9 Copying and pasting means you can copy the best 'take' of a section multiple times, rather than try to play it perfectly twice. You can also move recorded segments around on the timeline. And you can trim by dragging the yellow box that surrounds each segment.

10 Now add another instrument by pressing the '+' at the bottom left. This lets you select the type of instrument you want to record on the next track. Make sure you start in the right position on the timeline, and record.

11 As you build up your song, you can use the headphones icon next to a track to hear that track alone, or the crossed-out speaker icon to mute a track. These buttons allow you to concentrate on specific tracks.

WANT MORE? NanoStudio It'll cost you at £10.49, but more serious electronic musicians will love the more traditional layout, as well as the super handy MIDI editing.

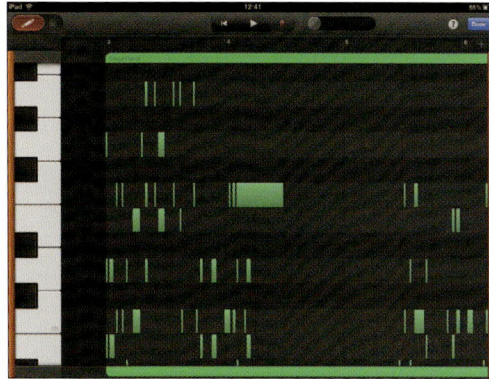

12 Another recently added feature in GarageBand is the Note Editor. We've already shown you how to copy and paste, but you can now finetune that best take you've made too. To do so, double-tap on a track, and a bubble will appear – tap 'Edit' on the far right of it.

13 You'll now see a keyboard layout of all the notes in that track. Use pinch-to-zoom gestures to swoop in on the notes you want to change: pinch from the centre to the sides to show more or less of the timeline on screen, or from the centre to the top and bottom to zoom in or out of particular octaves.

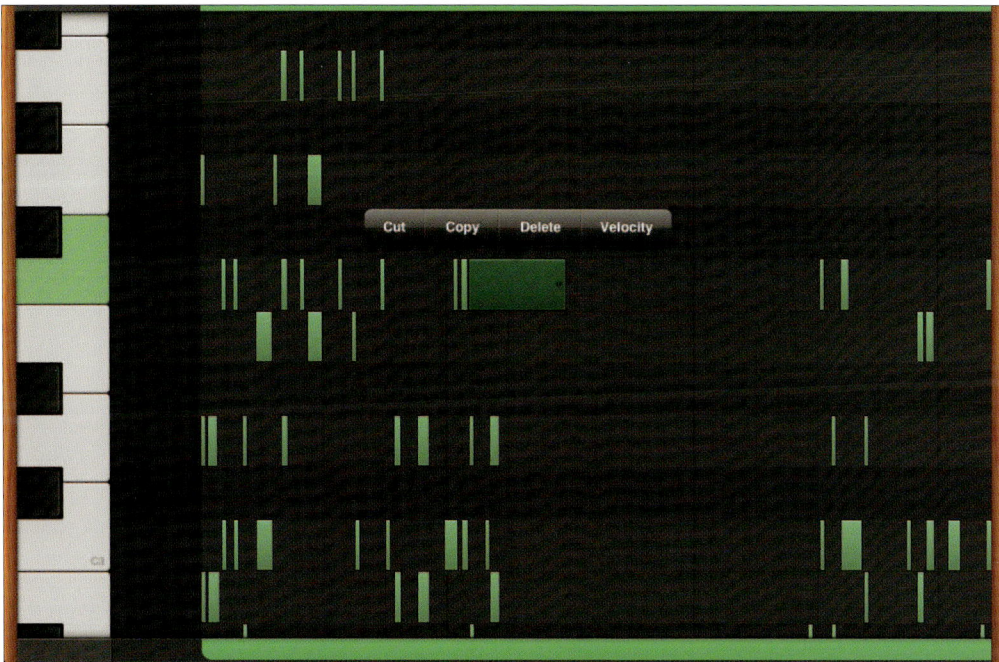

NEED TO KNOW
More track options

The icon at the top right (it looks like a set of EQ controls) lets you edit pan, echo, and reverb levels to the selected track – yet more options to add effects to your sounds.

14 Long-press on a note and you can move it in the timeline, or extend its duration by dragging the arrow symbol that appears at the end of it. Double-tap on the note, and you can cut, copy or delete it, as well as adjust its velocity.

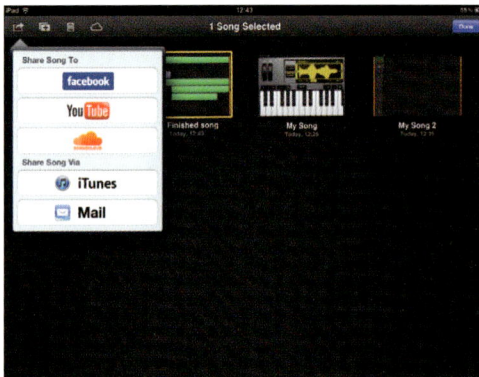

15 When you're done, it's time to share your song with the world. Tap the 'My Songs' button again. The view will zoom out. Tap the name of the song to type in your own name for it. Then tap 'Done', and long-press until the files start floating. Tap the song to highlight in orange, and hit the share icon in the top right corner to see your sharing options.

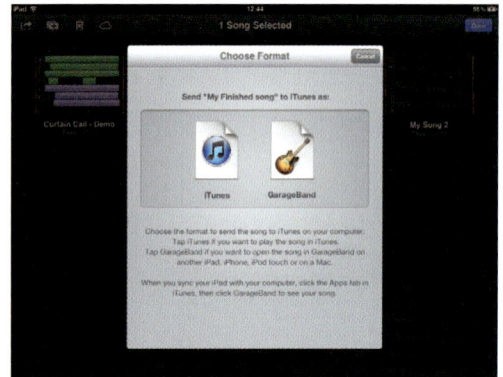

16 If you choose to send your song to iTunes, you'll be given the option to send it as a finalised AAC version, or as a GarageBand project that you can continue to edit on your Mac. However, you can also now send the AAC file via email from the same window, as well as immediately upload it to Facebook, YouTube or Soundcloud.

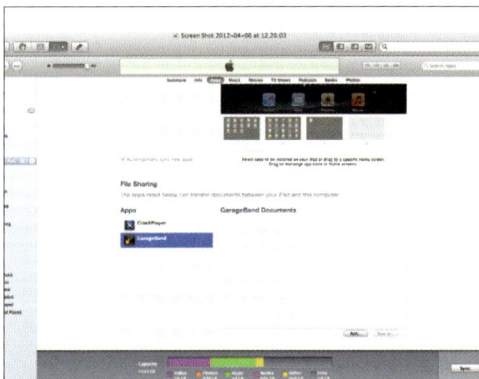

17 Next time you plug your iPad into your computer, head to iTunes and click on your iPad in the source list, then click the 'Apps' tab. Scroll down to 'File Sharing'. Click on 'GarageBand' from the list of apps that appears, and you'll see your song displayed, along with an option to save it.

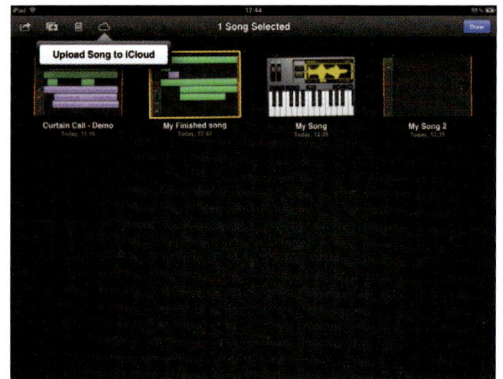

18 You can also send to iCloud by tapping the cloud icon instead of the arrow. For your next project, you can also select songs you're working on using other devices via iCloud. In My Songs, select the '+' icon at the top left, and a pane to import projects will appear. Turn the 'Use iCloud' switch on and you'll be able to transfer without fiddly cables.

Jam together

Since GarageBand for iPad first launched last year, Apple has added some great new features, the best of which is Jam Session, which lets you hook up and play live with other iOS devices, even recording a take. Here, we show you how...

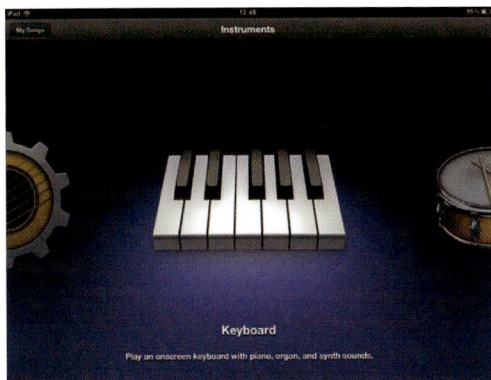

1 You can connect with up to three other iOS devices (Any iPad, iPhone 4 or 4S and iPod Touch fourth generation) to play live together. Either start a new song or select the instrument you want to play in an existing song: make sure you and all your friends all have your Bluetooth turned on, or that you're connected to the same WiFi network.

2 To start a jam session with a bunch of your friends, tap the Jam Session button next to the settings icons in the top right-hand corner of the screen. If one of your friends has already created a session, you'll be able to select it from the drop-down list that appears. Otherwise, choose to 'Create Session' to start a new jam yourself.

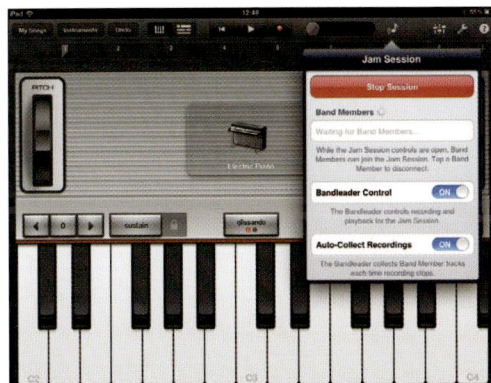

3 Your friends will appear in the drop-down list as they join – though you can remove them with a tap if you so choose. By default, the session's creator will collect all the recordings you and your friends make at the end of the session and have them appear on their project, but you can turn this off by flicking the switch next to 'Auto-Collect Recordings'.

4 Just start playing! You'll all play in the same key signature and tempo, and if you were the person who created the session, you can start recording it at any time as you normally would. Once you've all finished jamming, stop the recording, and all the tracks will appear on your iPad for post-editing. Simple!

Social network on the go with Facebook for iPad

▶ For the world's biggest social network, Facebook has been remarkably slow on the uptake with iPad. Founder Mark Zuckerberg famously declared that the iPad wasn't "mobile", and a dedicated Facebook app only launched 18 months after the first-generation iPad went on sale.

But Facebook has made up for lost time: the native iPad app is every bit as polished as the iPhone version, letting you chat while surfing, share content and more. It's even been freshly updated for the super sharp Retina display resolution, so it's easy on the eyes too.

VITAL INFO

We show you how to get to grips with the world's most popular social network, newly improved for the Retina Display on the new iPad.

What you need
Facebook app (Free from the App Store)
A Facebook account

Time required
20 minutes

News Feed

This is the main interface, which drops you straight into your news stream. All Facebook features can be accessed from the menu button in the top left.

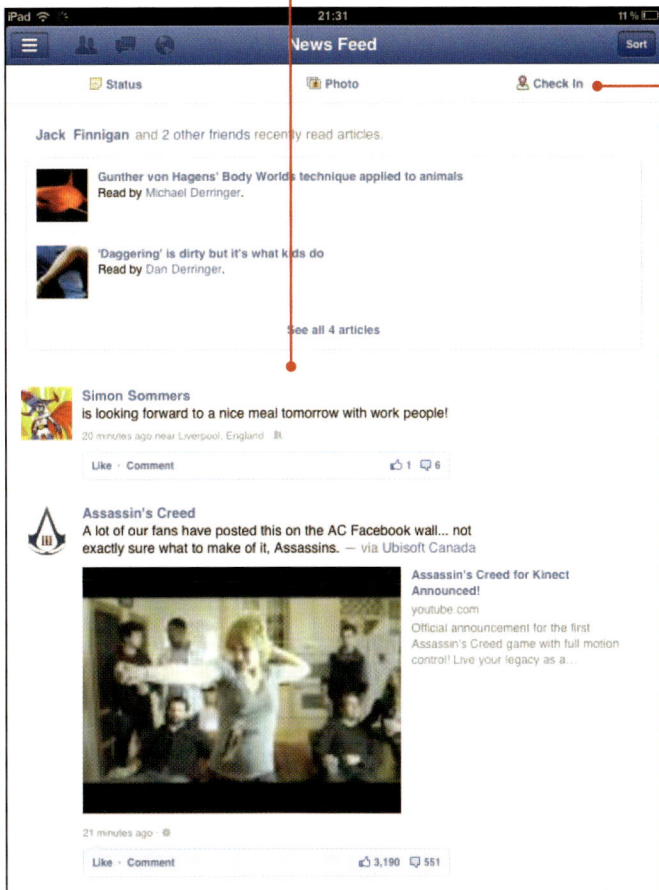

Send out a blast

From this screen, you can simply tap Status to write an update, tap Photo to upload an image or even check-in at a location.

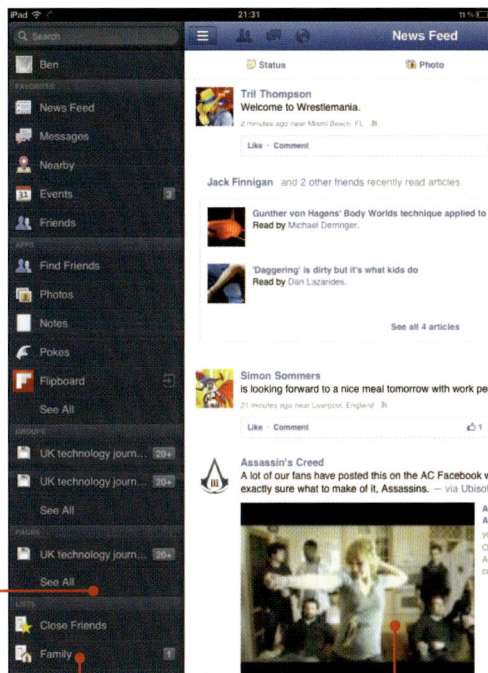

Easy access

All your services and apps are on the left hand side.

Swipe to shut

To close the sidebar, just swipe to the left.

Stay inside

Videos and web links all open within the app.

Step-by-step guide)))

2 Head to settings in the Sidebar and choose Privacy Settings. You can then edit what you share and with whom, making every public or making sure only your friends have access.

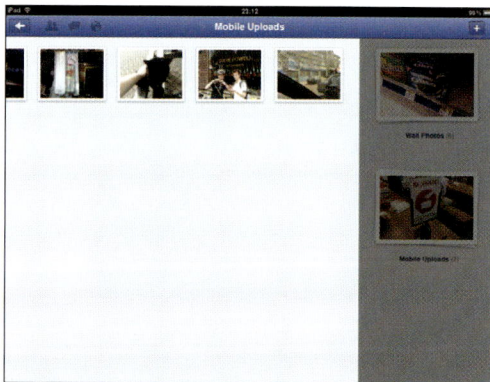

1 Download the Facebook app from the App Store and tap on the icon to launch. You'll be met with a simple screen: either log in with your details, or choose to sign up for a new account. You can log out at any time, and your details will be saved so you can quickly sign in again.

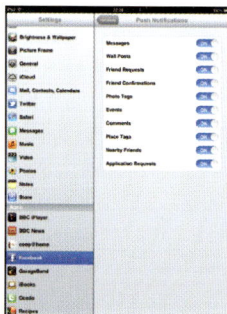

3 Sitting above your News Feed in the sidebar is your own profile. You can't edit it, but you can check out all your photos: tap to expand, pinch to zoom in, and pinch all the way out to close the image again.

EXPERT TIP

Choose to allow Facebook to send you push notifications, and you'll see a bubble in the corner of the app's homescreen icon letting you know how many notifications you've received. You can tweak what these are in Settings; better still, you can see them at any time by pulling down the Notification Centre tray from the top of the screen.

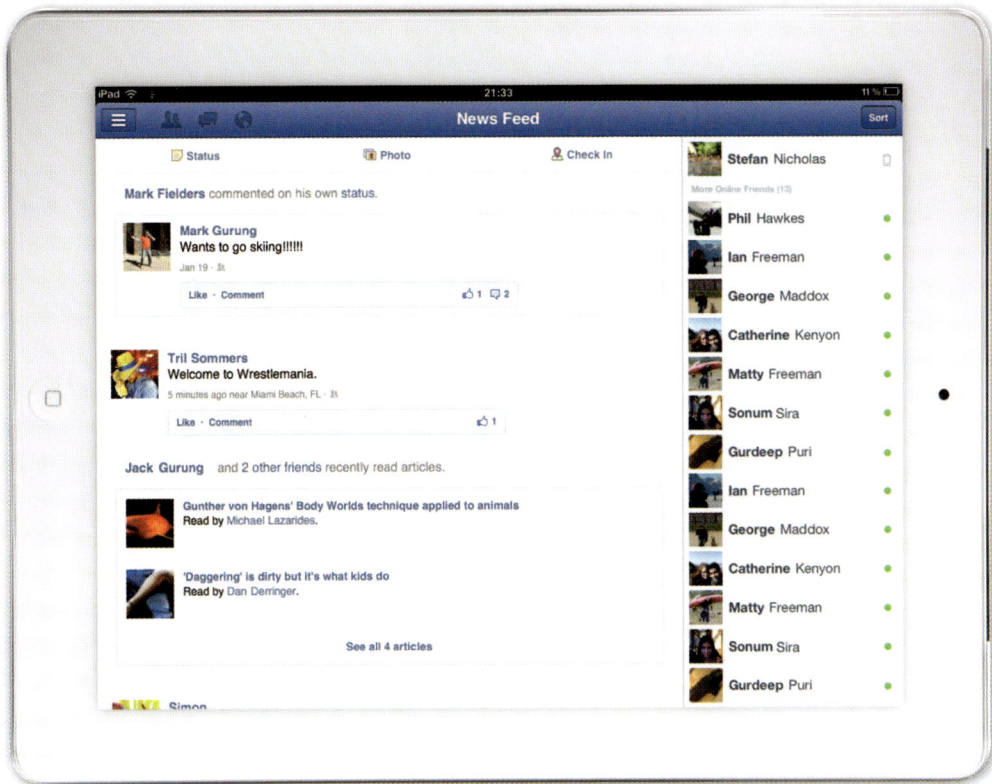

4 You won't see Facebook Chat in the Sidebar of services, but that's only because it's right next to the newsfeed. Anyone with a green icon is online to chat, and you can carry on conversations from anywhere in the app. The only problem? You can only see it's there in the first place when you're holding the iPad in landscape mode.

5 Three more icons along the top let you see friend requests, messages and notifications in drop-down windows, while the Status button just below lets you tap out a message, add a link, location or image, and even choose who you share it with.

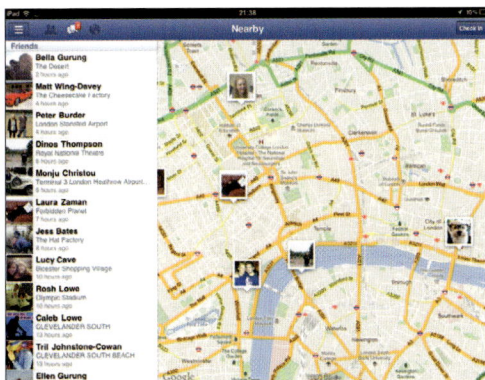

6 You can check-in straight from the News Feed, but head to the Nearby feature and you can see your where your friends have checked in around you on a convenient Google Map of your location.

Tweet from your iPad with Twitter

▶ The Twitter app started life as an iPhone app called Tweetie, which was made by a third-party developer called Atebits. Twitter (the company) was so impressed with the way Tweetie brought Twitter's features to mobile devices that it bought it, rebranded it, and made it into its own, official Twitter client.

Now there's a dedicated iPad version: a simple, elegant piece of software that makes it incredibly easy to tweet on the go. It allows you to post pictures, videos, and locations, as well as making it easy to interact with other users through hashtags and @replies. And with two cameras on the iPad 2 and new iPad, the potential for sharing images and videos on the move is huge. Here's how to tweet on your iPad.

VITAL INFO

We show you how to get involved with the hottest social network on the planet from the comfort of your iPad.

What you need
Your iPad
Twitter app (free from the App Store)
A Twitter account

Time required
10 minutes

Stream of tweets

This is the main interface. You can select to view tweets from your Timeline, tweets that mention you (@replies), and Direct Messages. You can also select to view your profile lists.

Write your thoughts

At any point, you can tap this compose icon to fire off a tweet. Tweets must be under 140 characters long – a character count pops up when you start typing.

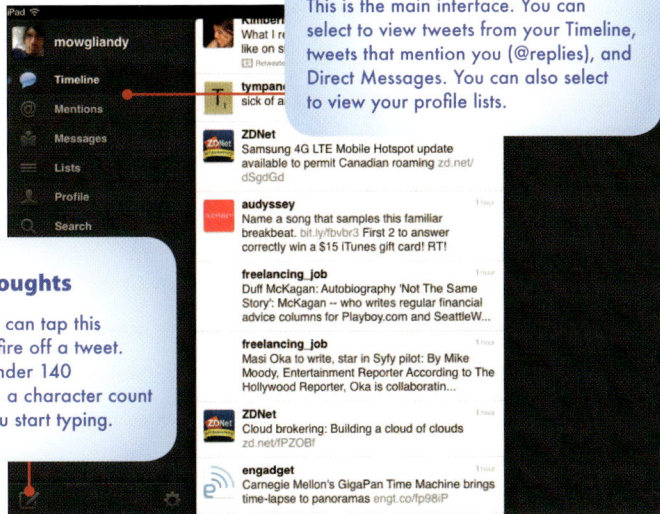

All in one

The app interface will show links, photos, and even play YouTube clips, with no need to leave the app.

Back and forth

Once you've read the webpage, slide it to the right so it moves out of the way. Swipe it right again to get rid of it completely.

Web within

The app has a sliding interface. Tap a link in a tweet to open it, and all the other columns slide to the left to reveal a web browser.

Step-by-step guide ❱❱❱

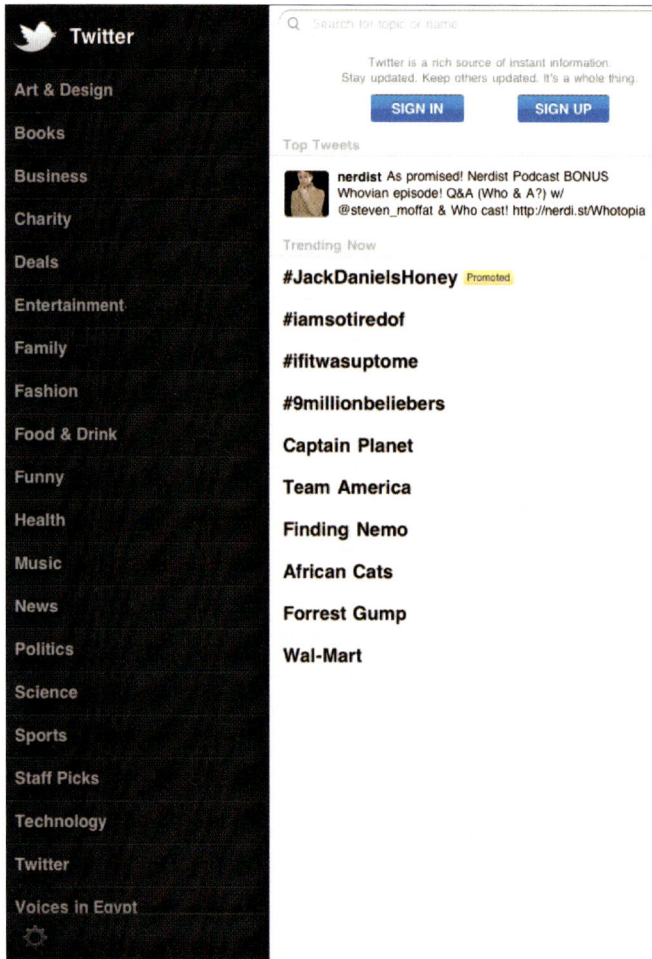

1 Download the Twitter app and open it up. The first screen tells you, somewhat vacuously, that Twitter is "a whole thing". Ignore that and check out what people are currently saying about the subjects of the moment by tapping the Trending Now topics – or look through aggregated posts on particular topics on the left.

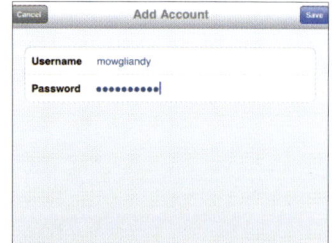

2 If you don't have an account, you can sign up to Twitter from inside the app. Press 'Sign up' and fill out the form. If you already have an account, you can simply tap 'Sign in' and enter your username and password.

3 When you've signed in, you'll be asked if you want Twitter to use your current location. This information can be added to tweets. You'll also be asked if you want Twitter to 'push' updates to you as they happen.

EXPERT TIP

From the Advanced settings screen, you can install a bookmark in Safari that allows you to easily send links from Safari to the Twitter app for sharing. It involves a bit of fiddling with bookmarks in Safari, but the instructions are all there when you press the 'Install Safari Bookmarklet' button in Twitter's settings.

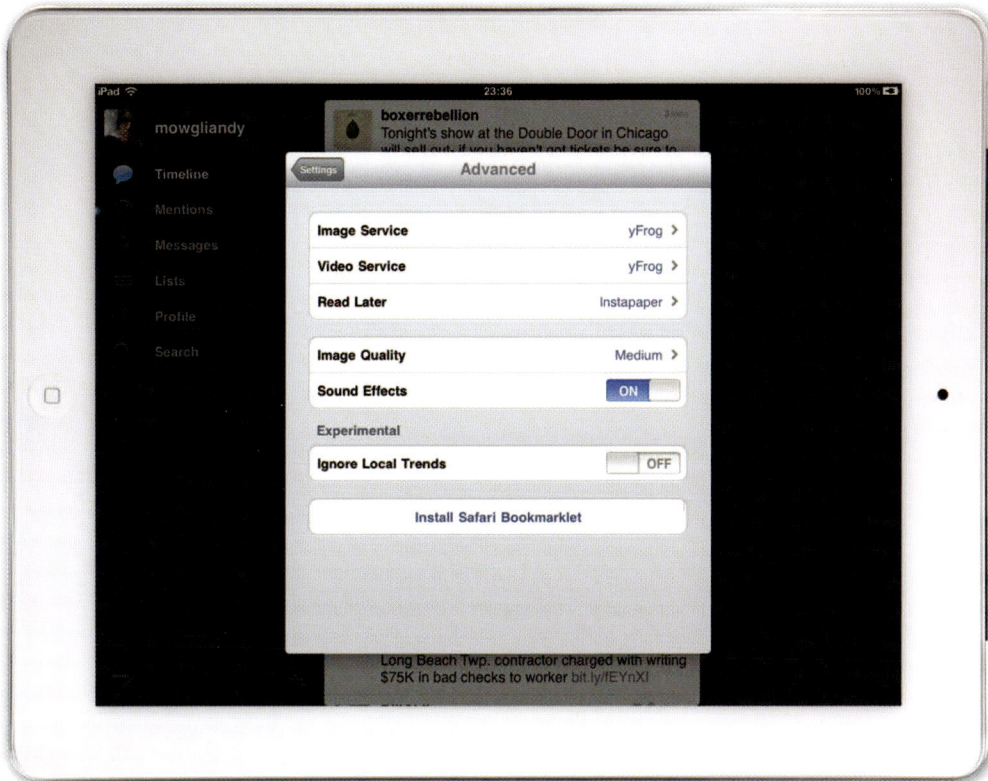

4 Tap the cog icon to go to Settings. Tap 'Advanced' to set your preferences for sharing pictures and videos – your picture-sharing service is set to use yFrog by default, but there are loads of other services to choose from.

WANT MORE?
TweetDeck

The Twitter app is great for Twitter, but if you want to add Facebook into the mix, all from one app, try TweetDeck (free). This app allows you to input your Facebook details and manage both networks from the same place.

5 When you have all your settings just as you like them, you're ready to tweet. Tap the compose icon (bottom left) and type away. Tap the camera icon to add a picture. The compass symbol embeds your location in the tweet.

6 Finally, tap the '@' sign to choose people to send the tweet to. A list appears and you can simply select your friends from the list. The hash sign lets you add a 'hashtag' – a symbol that makes your tweet easy to search for.

Tablet to order: The best supermarket apps for your iPad

▶ We're in a post-PC world, claims Apple, and the iPad is leading the way. But for the revolution to truly succeed, we all need to be able to manage the activities we once relied on PCs for just as easily on a tablet.

Ordering the weekly shop is one of those more mundane tasks. But with the vivid screen of the new iPad and the right apps, it actually becomes anything but a chore. We look at three apps from the App Store that won't just get your shopping list crossed off, but will have your taste buds tingling too…

VITAL INFO

We look at the best iPad apps for shopping on the go – and getting your groceries delivered right to your door.

What you need
A credit or debit card

Time required
30 minutes

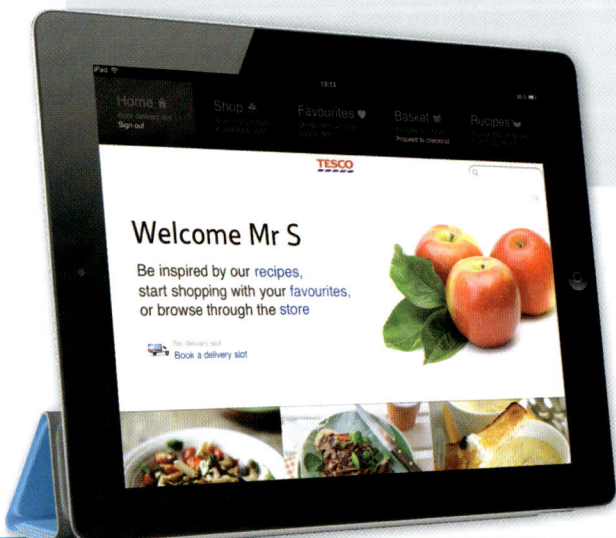

Step-by-step guide ▶▶▶

Ocado

Ocado is the famous home delivery company that carries Waitrose produce right to your door, and it was first on the scene with an app especially made for iPad.

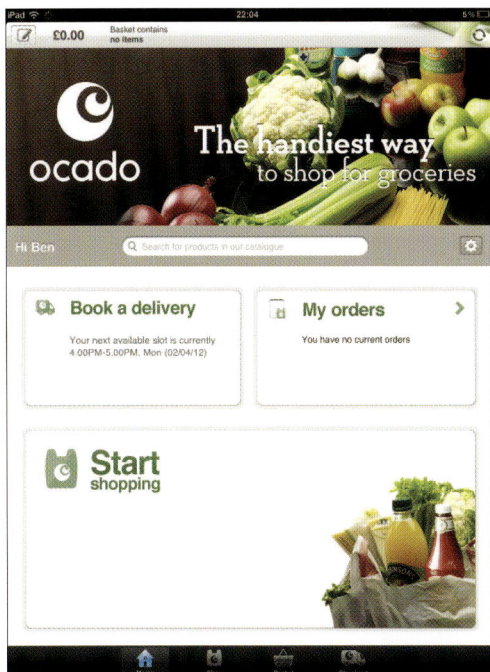

1 Install and open the Ocado app. The homescreen provides access to everything you need, from information about the price of your basket to quick links to order. Navigation is via four buttons at the bottom of the screen – or by hitting the big Start Shopping icon.

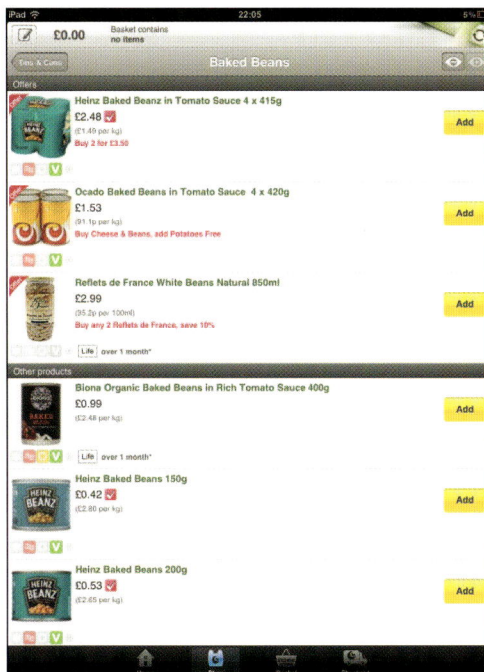

2 Browse through the categories to see what's on offer, and stick it in your basket by tapping the yellow Add icon – handy images accompany every item. Navigate back by tapping the arrow in the top left corner of the screen, or open a shopping list virtual memo pad with the pencil icon directly above that.

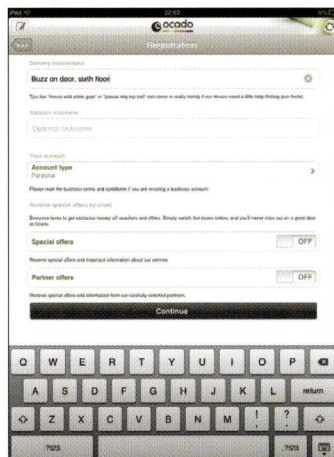

3 Hit the basket to checkout and book a time or delivery. During the registration process you can specify extra details so the man in the van knows where to find you. And that's it!

Tesco Recipes

The name's almost misleading. Tesco Recipes is a full-on shopping app, just like Ocado for iPad, but it's stuffed full of inspiration too by way of delicious recipe suggestions and a gorgeous layout.

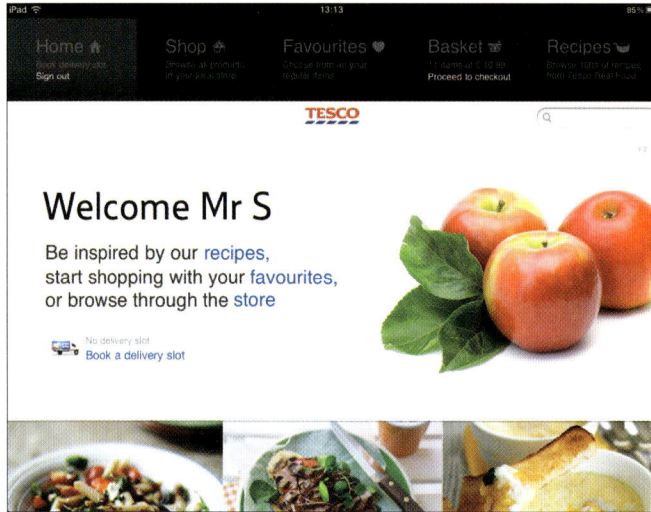

1 Open the app and register: you'll land on a splash homepage. Tap the Tesco logo and you'll see the various services can be accessed via the large icons along the top, while the main section lets you see your basket, schedule a delivery and even amend your order.

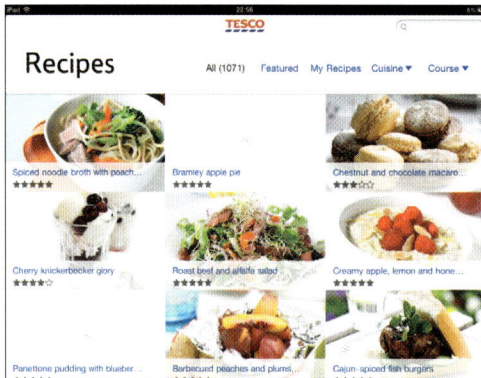

2 Hit the Recipes section for a menu of mouth-watering dishes, complete with a user review star-rating. Click on these for simple instructions, and if you like what you see, one tap will instantly let you add the necessary ingredients to your basket.

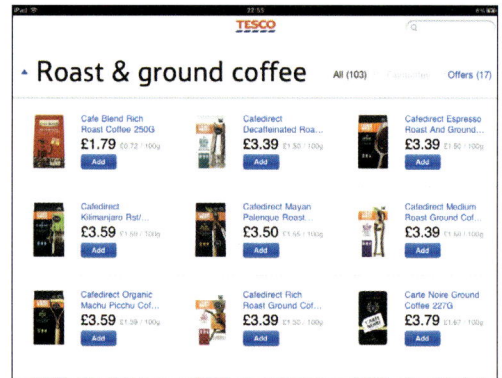

3 You can also go à la carte, and shop for whatever you need. Whatever virtual shelf you're browsing, tap the Offers tab in the top right corner of the screen to see what relevant deals you can save money on right now.

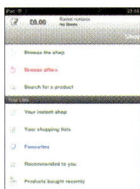

EXPERT TIP

Both Tesco and Ocado cut prices viciously to stay competitive. In fact, the latter promises a Tesco price match, although be sure to shop around, as both offer regular deals on items, as you'd see in-store. Delivery charges for both vary by time and date, and sign-on deals can also vary: Ocado, for instance, gives you £10 off your first shop.

Amazon Windowshop

Amazon's iPad-exclusive app makes full use of the big screen to let you browse through categories and handpick items. It's not just books and DVDs, though: you can do your weekly shop this way too!

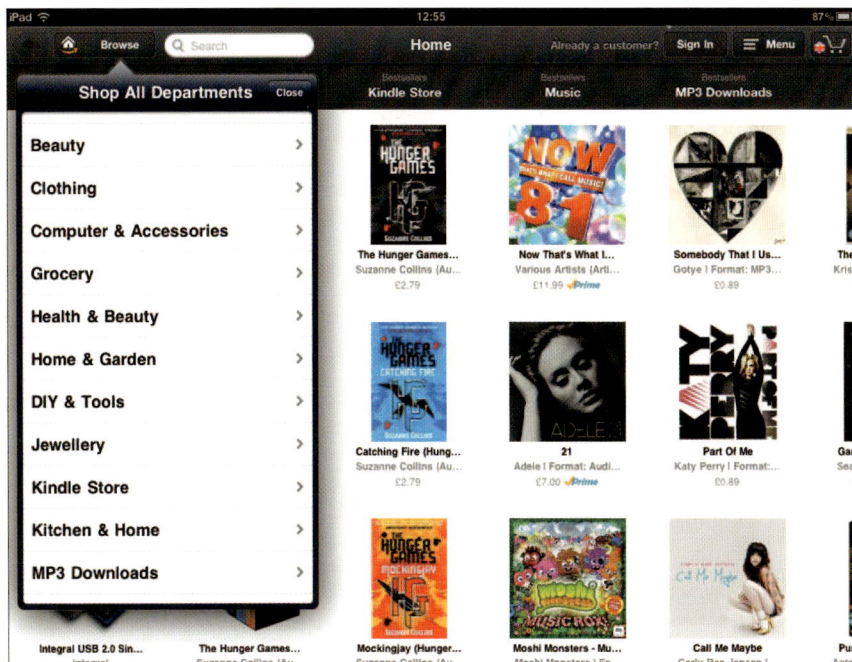

1 Download and open the app. You'll be met with a grid of Amazon's most popular categories, but don't worry: groceries are here too. Just tap the Browse button in the top right, tap Grocery and you'll see the sub-categories and everything on offer appear.

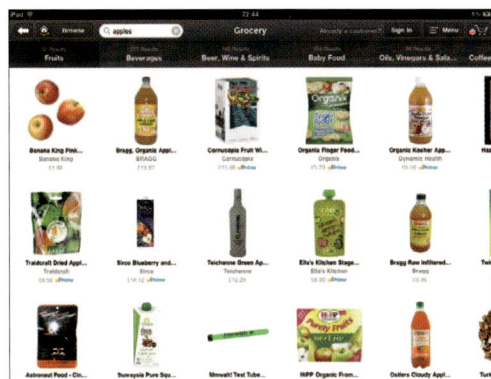

2 Each time you tap a category column, the list expands into more columns, with a big image accompanying every item so you can see what you're getting. If you need to go back at any time, the back button is in the top right-hand corner of the screen.

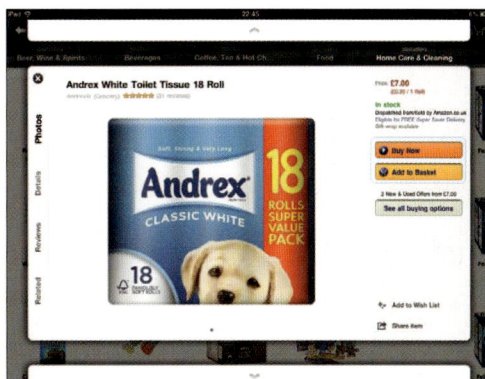

3 Click on an item to expand it. If you're signed in, you can buy with one tap, but otherwise click to add it to your shopping basket, which can be accessed from the trolley icon in the top right of the screen at any time.

WANT MORE?
Morrisons

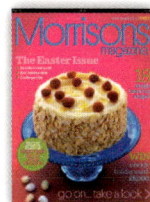

Morrisons' free iPad magazine has some clever tricks up its sleeve. Great features, recipes and instructional videos are accompanied by genius additions such as an on-screen timer, so you'll know when your food is done.

Edit and organise images using iPhoto

▶ Mac users have been managing and editing their photo library using iPhoto for years. Now Apple has brought iPhoto to the iPad – and at the low price of just £2.99. It may lack the power and scope of a desktop editing app like Photoshop or Aperture, but iPhoto for iPad is still an impressive tool: simple to use, yet capable of transforming poor shots into eye-catchers. It will also help you keep an unruly collection of photos in line – and won't keep you chained to your desk while you're doing it. Here's our guide to getting the best out of the app.

VITAL INFO

We'll show you how to edit your photos for more professional results. You'll also find out how to organise and share snaps to show off your handiwork!

What you need
Your iPad 2 or new iPad
iPhoto app
Some images to edit

Time required
1 hour

Welcome to Pages
The most beautiful word processor ever designed for a mobile device.

Life in the Serengeti

Continue

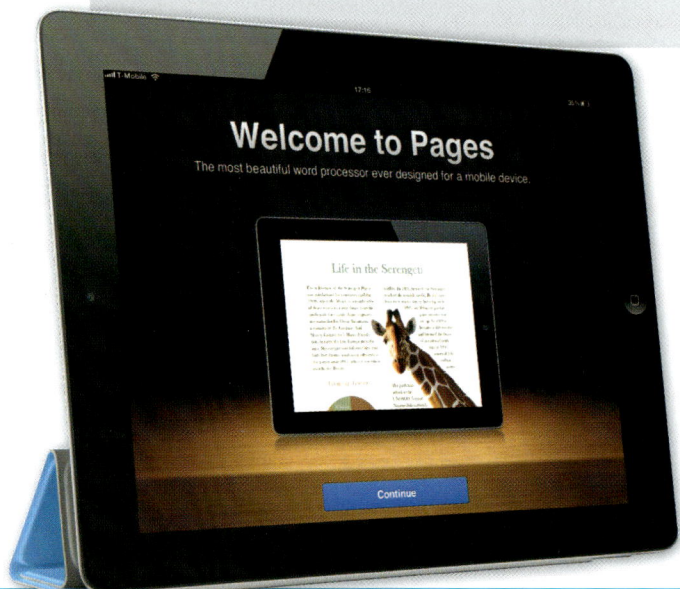

Step-by-step guide ❱❱❱

EDITING PHOTOS

1 Editing a photo couldn't be simpler. When viewing the shot in iPhoto, tap the 'Edit' button at the top right. This brings up an icon-filled bar at the bottom of the screen, with five advanced editing tools on the left and five simple tools in the middle. Remember that 'Undo' always removes your last step!

SIMPLE EDITING

2 If you don't have time for in-depth editing, tap the Auto-Enhance icon, which will adjust exposure and colour and eliminate red-eye in a matter of seconds. There are also buttons to rotate the shot 90 degrees, flag it for later editing, mark it as a favourite or hide it so that it won't show in your library.

ADVANCED EDITING – CROP AND STRAIGHTEN

3 This tool allows you to crop an image. Just drag the box to select the desired portion. You can retain the original aspect ratio by toggling the icon in the bottom right. You can also straighten wonky photos by turning the dial at the bottom.

EXPOSURE

4 Here you can adjust brightness and contrast, either for the entire shot or for the brightest and darkest areas individually. Drag the icons on the bottom bar to adjust, or place your finger on the shot and move according to the tool tip.

COLOUR

5 This is the tool for jazzing up or toning down colour. The left slider adjusts the saturation for added vibrancy or neutrality, while the others are individually tailored to adjust greens, blues and skin tones. These can also be tweaked by placing a finger on the screen and dragging up, down, left or right. White balance can be adjusted using the icon at the bottom right.

BRUSHES

6 Want to adjust an area rather than the whole photo? Brushes let you sharpen, soften, lighten, darken, saturate or desaturate small sections, as well as eliminating ugly red-eye and gently scrubbing away skin blemishes. The eraser icon lets you remove any brush effect, while the 'detect edges' icon applies the brush effect only to a 'block' of colour and lightness, not the entire area your fingertip touches.

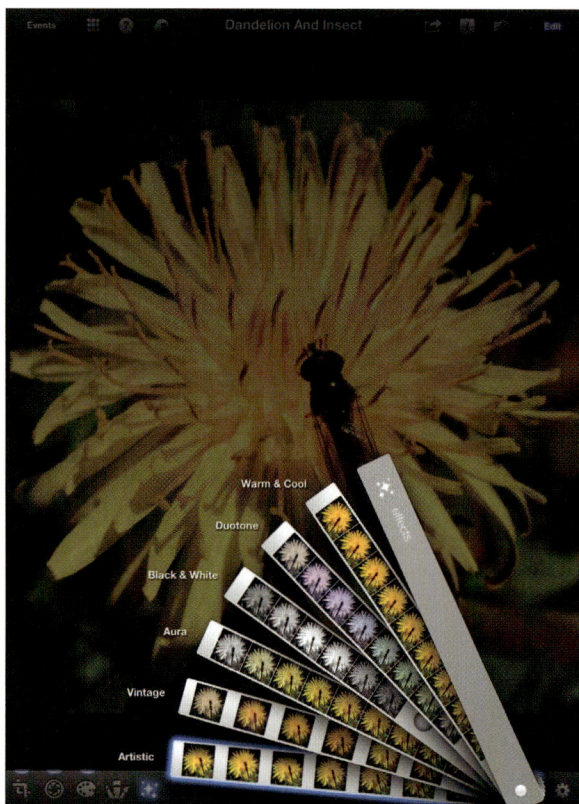

EFFECTS

7 Clearly inspired by iPhone apps like Instagram and Hipstamatic, 'Effects' lets you apply arty filters to shots, changing their whole look in an instant. Simply tap the starry Effects tab and you'll bring up swatches of clever effects. The Artistic mode turns your photo into a watercolour, Aura isolates strong colours, making them the focus of the picture and turning the rest black and white. Vintage creates a '70s faded acetate effect. Play around with them to get the best look for your photo before you print or share by uploading to an online gallery or Facebook.

Organise and share your photos

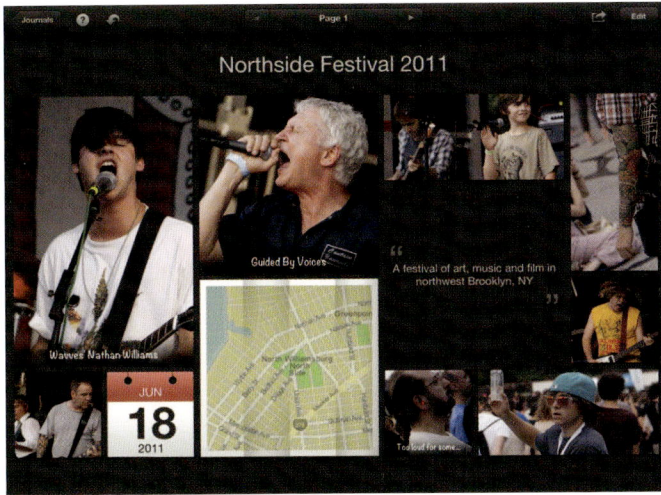

JOURNALS

8 These are pages in which you can group photos with other info to tell the 'story' of an event or holiday. Shots can be reshaped and dragged into place, and you can group them with maps, blocks of text, quotes, weather info and more. When you're happy with the layout, they can be exported to the web via iCloud or iTunes.

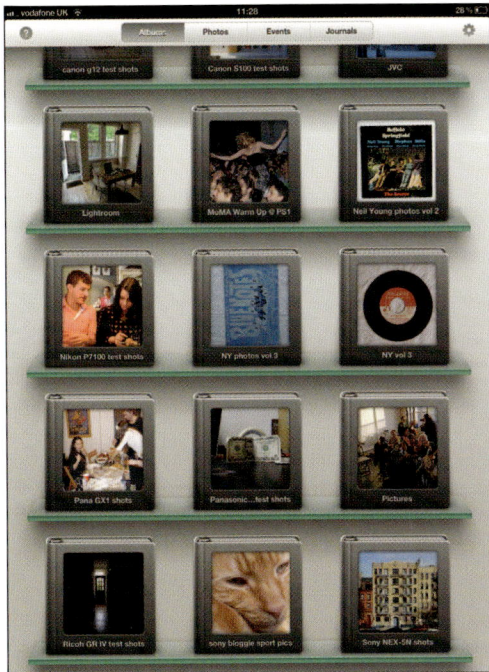

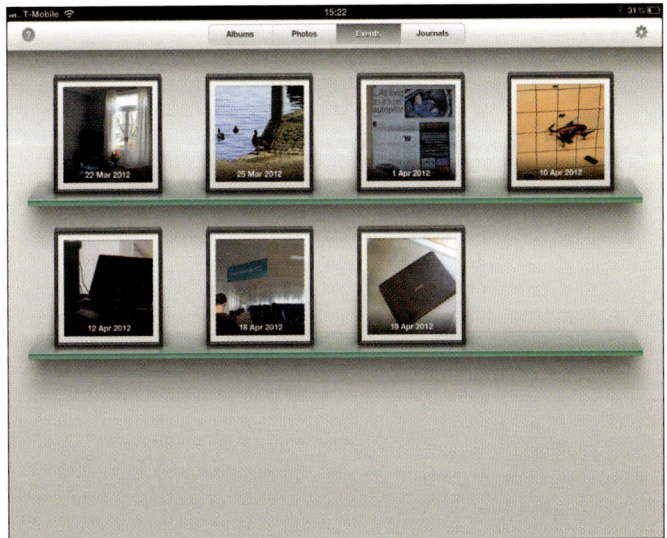

ALBUMS

9 Albums are collections of photos, automatically generated by iPhoto. Photos are grouped by marker (favourite or flag), and whether or not they have been edited. There are albums for your iPad's entire Camera Roll, every photo you've imported yourself, and the last import you made. You cannot create your own albums, but you can choose the 'key photo' for each of them.

EVENTS

10 Another way of grouping and organising shots, Events uses the timestamp on photos to group them together by the date on which they were taken. Events, Albums and individual shots can be shared quickly via email, Twitter, Facebook, Flickr or iTunes, or printed by tapping a single button.

Make and edit films with iMovie

▶ The new iPad's razor-sharp 9.7 inch Retina display is absolutely perfect for watching videos, and the extra graphics power you get from the tablet's new A5X processor makes editing them incredibly easy too – especially now that Apple's feature-packed video app, iMovie, has made its way to the iPad from the Mac.

iMovie for iPad launched last year with the iPad 2, but it's had a few updates since then – and to complement the new iPad's 1080p high-def camera, you can now edit in Full HD too. Here, we show you how to do it like a pro.

VITAL INFO

We'll show you how to edit clips, weave together a polished home video and even make a Hollywood-style trailer - all in 1080p full HD!

What you need
Your new iPad
Clips you've shot to play around with

Time required
1 hour

Clip list

Everything you've shot on your iPad, or imported via iTunes, will appear here. You can also choose from the images in your Photo album.

Preview

See what you're editing while you work. Just tap the Play triangle to view your current build.

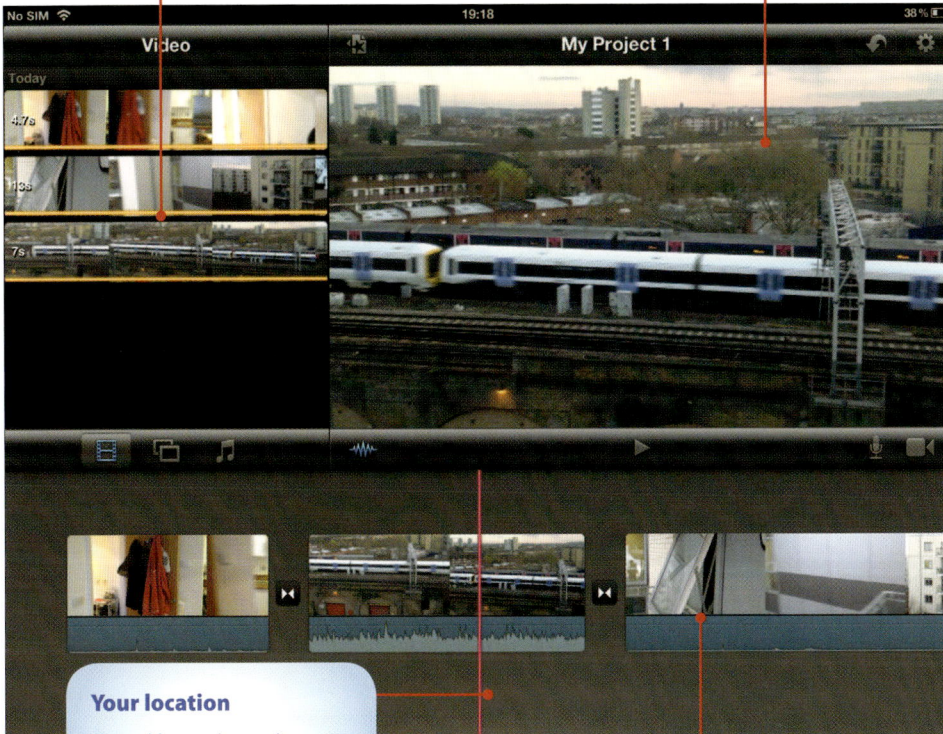

Your location

The red line in the timeline shows the frame you're working on. Tap or swipe to move it.

The Timeline

Shows all the different tracks included in your edit, including audio. The triangles in boxes show and let you edit transitions.

NEED TO KNOW
Importing movies into iMovie

iMovie offers some powerful editing features, but the flipside is that it's rather restrictive about the types of footage it opens. You can see what formats it supports opposite, but do be aware that many cameras shoot video in a format, such as AVCHD, that requires conversion first, so be sure to check what yours does before splashing out on the £25 Camera Connection Kit.

You can convert most formats using iMovie on a desktop computer, or by using the free Handbrake software (*www.handbrake.fr*) for PC, Mac and Linux. To edit video filmed on any other iOS device, just hook them up to the same computer with iTunes and transferring the video via USB cable. Note that the only other iOS device that will be able to open 1080p footage you've shot on the new iPad is an iPhone 4S, however.

Step-by-step guide ❯❯❯

Mastering iMovie basics

iMovie makes it a breeze to run video clips together, trim them and move them around. Here we show you how to create your first iMovie project by getting to grips with the app's easy-to-use features.

WANT MORE?
Avid Studio for iPad

For £2.99, Avid Studio is a bit more professional than iMovie, with more advanced tools including picture in picture editing. The downside is that it doesn't yet support 1080p output on the new iPad.

1 After the splash screen, choose to create a new project. The middle bar lets you choose videos, images or music to insert into the timeline with a double-tap, or shoot video from the app with the camera icon on the far right.

2 You can move clips around in the timeline with a long press and drag. To edit the transitions, double-tap to choose the type and length of transition, or tap once and then on the yellow arrow below to edit the transition frame by frame.

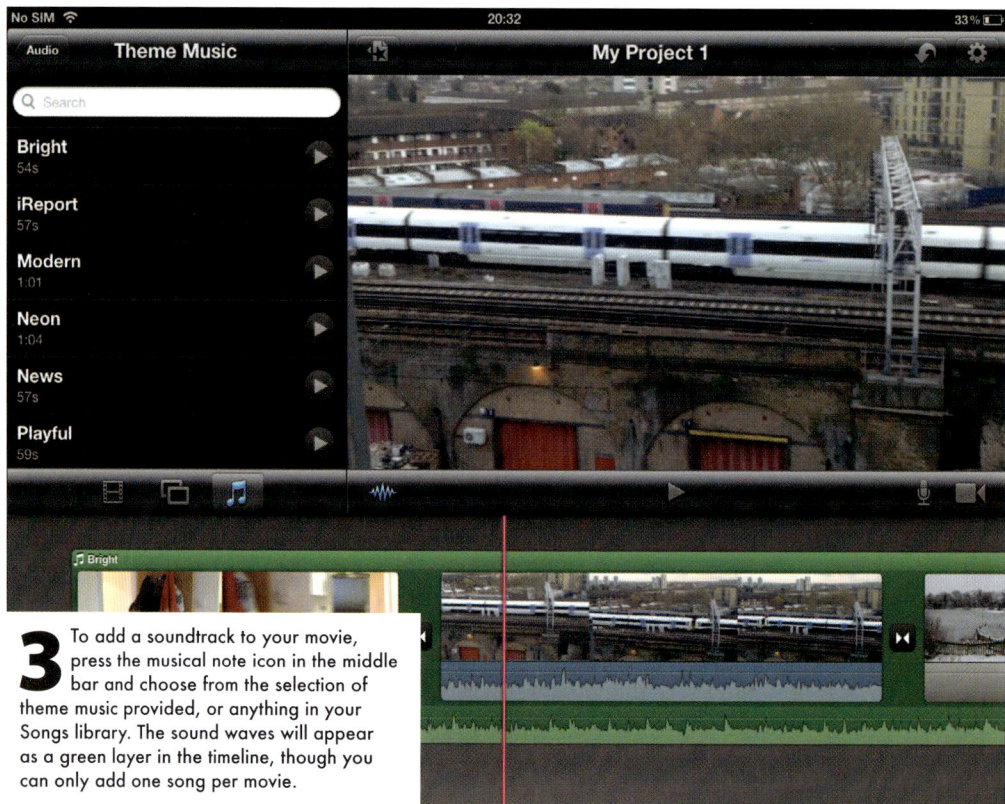

3 To add a soundtrack to your movie, press the musical note icon in the middle bar and choose from the selection of theme music provided, or anything in your Songs library. The sound waves will appear as a green layer in the timeline, though you can only add one song per movie.

Make your own movie trailer

1 iMovie now lets you create fun Hollywood-style trailers from clever templates. From the start screen, choose the '+' symbol, then New Project. You can preview samples of nine different genres on the next screen. Click Create when you find one you like.

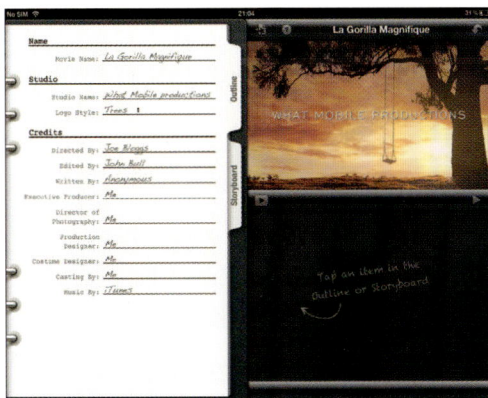

2 In the Outline tab, you can click the various fields to fill in the credits that will appear on the trailer, and give your movie a name. For added authenticity, you can even provide the name of a mock production company.

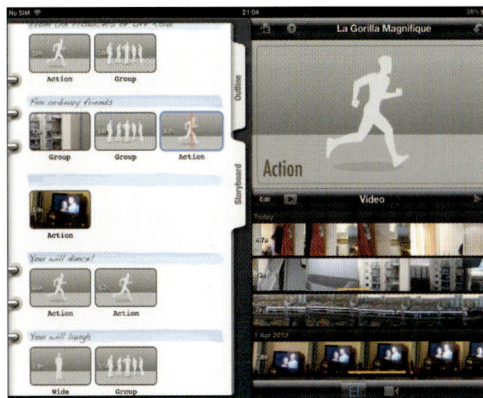

3 Click the Storyboard tab to fill in segments – each one shows its length and action required. Click a shot, and you can film it in the top right pane. Alternatively, click the film icon at the bottom right, and you can select a segment from previously-recorded footage.

NEED TO KNOW

Exporting your film couldn't be easier. From the start screen, hit the share button along the bottom (the one with the arrow). Hitting Camera Roll will let you save it onto the iPad's storage at any resolution of your choice, including 1080p. Alternatively, you can send it directly to YouTube, facebook, Vimeo or CNN iReport from the same pane.

Celebrate London 2012 in style on your iPad, as we bring you our pick of the apps that are going for gold

Ultimate Olympic apps

Summer Games 3D
From Free

Available in a free 'Lite' version as well as the 69p full edition, this game features no fewer than 20 events (three in Lite) that'll put your fingers through their paces – you furiously tap to build up speed. The visuals aren't fantastic, but there's no other game that brings such a variety of events to the iPad.

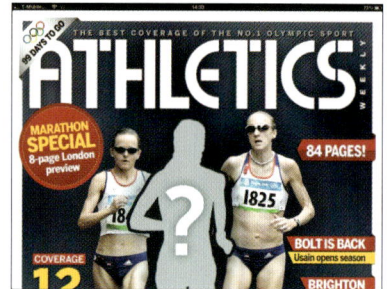

Athletics Weekly
Free (in-app purchases required)

The world's premier athletics magazine is now available on the iPad – perfect for the build-up to the 2012 Games. A monthly subscription costs £5.49, or you can feast your eyes on a year's worth of issues for £57.99. You'll also get access to an archive of over 200 back issues.

BMW iMagazine
Free

BMW, a chief sponsor to the British Olympic team, has produced this slick interactive magazine in the run-up to the Games. It's heavily branded, but there's some nice content, including video clips and interviews with team members past and present.

Eurosport Player
Free

Eurosport is one of the broadcasters covering London 2012 – and this iPad app lets you keep an eye on events wherever you happen to be. The app itself is free, but you'll need to pay a subscription fee of £2.99 per month to watch live broadcasts.

London 2012 Trivia Quiz
£0.69

Pub quiz addicts will lap up this app, packed with trivia questions about this year's Games. Want to know how long it took to build the stadium, or whether this year's new event is Women's Boxing, Men's Snooker or Women's Football? Find out here.

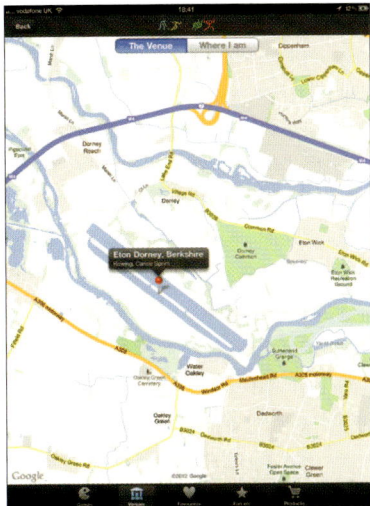

Londinium

Free

Similar to the iLondon 2012 app but available free of charge, Londinium isn't quite as stable or well made but still comes stuffed with useful information about both the Olympics and the Paralympics. There's a countdown clock, news feed (with a quick link to Twitter activity concerning the Games) and schedule for every sport, with Google Map shortcuts taking you instantly to every venue.

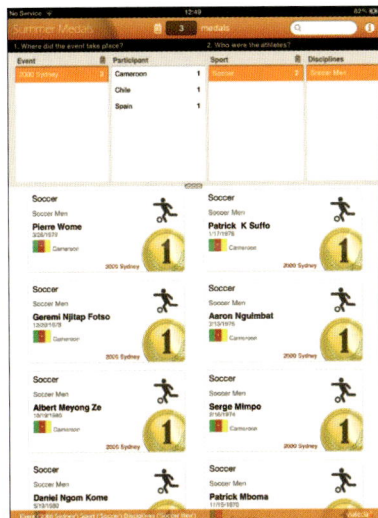

Summer Medals

Free

One for would-be Olympic historians, this is a simple, free and easy-to-search database of every gold, silver and bronze medal winner from every summer Olympic Games. Stats geeks will appreciate the info on offer, which could come in handy in all manner of Olympics-related quizzes.

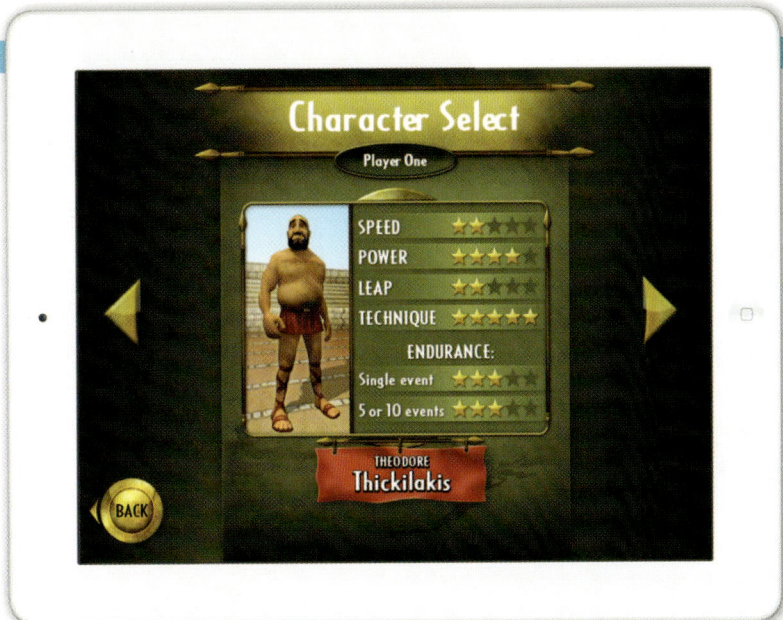

Spartan Athletics HD

£0.69

Get yourself into the Olympic spirit with this finger-straining recreation of the ancient Greek tournament. It features ten events (high jump, long jump, 100m, shot put, 110m hurdles, 1500m, javelin, discus, 400m and pole vault), several characters with different strengths and weaknesses, and the ability to play a friend on your iPad or via Bluetooth.

Ultimate 2012 Olympic Guide

£0.69

Packed to the gills with information, this guide has details of every venue and a handful of interviews with key athletes – including the world's fastest man, sprinter Usain Bolt. The daily agenda for the whole shebang should come in particularly handy, as it suggests potential highlight events – very handy if you need to ration your TV viewing time. It's not the most interactive of iPad magazines – you won't find any embedded video or fancy animations here – but some maps and other illustrations do offer touchscreen buttons to reveal extra information.

iLondon 2012

£1.49

It's easy to see why iLondon 2012 is one of the highest-ranked Olympics apps in the iTunes Store. It's slick and well produced, with Retina display-friendly visuals and no shortage of info on venues, competitors, events and the medals available. It'll aid your Olympic planning by scheduling events to your iPad's iCal calendar, and tell you how close you are to a particular venue using information from Google Maps. There's also a news feed harvesting updates from the official website, and during the Games the medal tracker will keep you up to speed on the current standings.

Create word processor documents with Pages

▶ One early criticism levelled at the iPad was that it was designed for consuming content rather than creating it. Pages is one of the apps that proves that claim wrong. It's a fully-featured word processor that not only lets you type text but create rich, visually-appealing documents with proper formatting and embedded images, charts and graphs. Not too shabby for £6.99.

While Pages is fairly straight-forward in its approach, the wealth of options on offer can be a little daunting for the new user. We've put together this guide to help you get started.

VITAL INFO

We'll explain how to create documents from scratch, or make use of readymade templates. You'll also learn how to lay out pages, import images and publish your docs via email or the web.

What you need
Your iPad
Pages app

Time required
1 hour

Welcome to Pages
The most beautiful word processor ever designed for a mobile device.

Life in the Serengeti

Continue

Step-by-step guide ▶▶▶

Master Pages in 10 easy steps

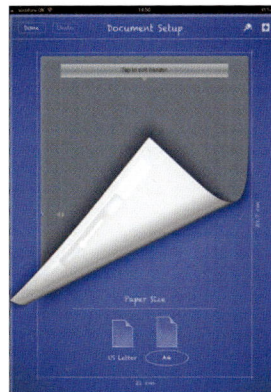

SETTING UP YOUR DOCUMENT

2 Hitting 'blank' presents you with an ominously empty sheet, but hit the spanner icon in the top right, then 'document setup', and you can choose the page size (A4 or US letter), set margins and edit the header and footer (page numbers and so on). These settings are retained for every page of your document.

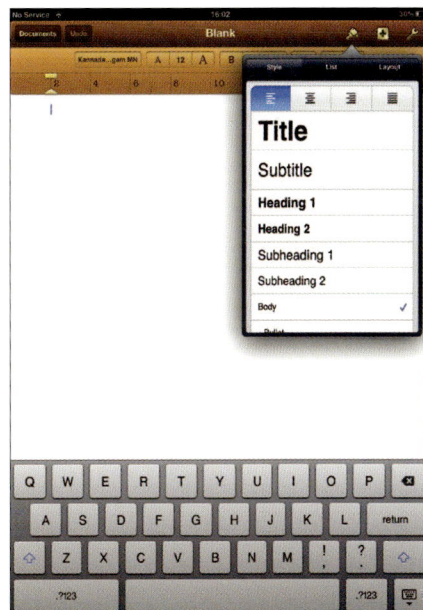

CREATING A NEW DOCUMENT

1 Hitting the '+' icon allows you to create a document (or import one from iTunes, iDisk or WebDAV). Pages comes with no fewer than 16 preset templates to give you a headstart at producing letters, CVs and the like – you simply swap the default and images with your own. For those who prefer a clean slate, there's a standard blank document too.

GETTING STARTED

3 Font settings and text justification can be tweaked using the icons in the top toolbar. If you want to keep things simple, tapping the brush icon also lets you swiftly select preset font sizes for titles, subtitles, headings, subheadings, bullet points, captions and labels (under 'Style'). You then type using the on-screen keypad, which works in both portrait and landscape.

Pages for iPad

Apple's word processor explained

Apple's word processor explained

Pages is a word processing app for the iPad, letting you construct documents with text, images, tables and more.

You can add charts and tables to your documents as well as pictures. For charts, you can even make them 3D, like the pie chart below. Tapping the 3D object lets you rotate and tilt it to make it that much more visually appealing.

● 2009 ● 2010 ● 2011 ● 2012
● 2013 ● 2014

7%
8%
10%
35%

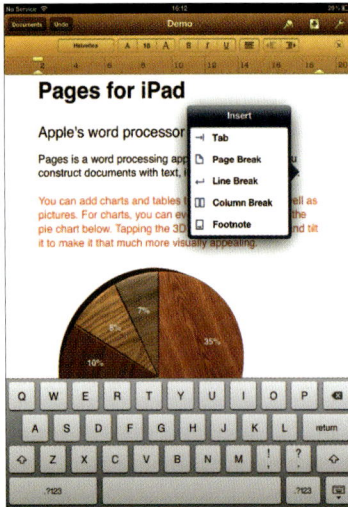

COLUMNS AND PAGE BREAKS

4 Hit the 'Format' brush icon, then 'Layout', and you'll see you can also create columns for your page (up to four), and adjust line spacing. For tabs, page breaks (start a new page), column breaks and footnotes, create an insertion point by tapping on the page at the desired spot, then selecting 'Insert'.

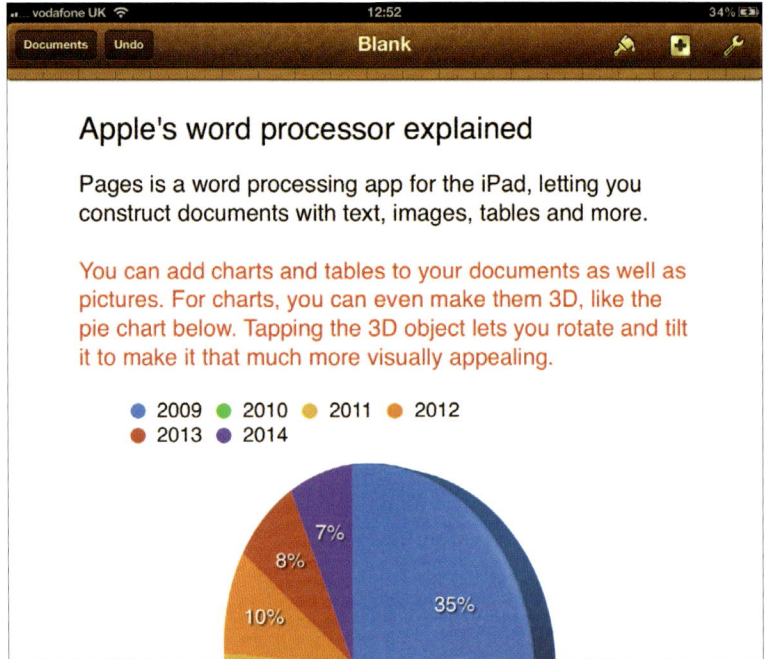

ADDING OBJECTS

5 Images, movies, charts and the like are called 'objects'. Hit the '+' button and you'll see there are four main categories: Media, Tables, Charts and Shapes. Media lets you add photos and video clips (these must be stored on your iPad), Tables and Charts are self-explanatory, while Shapes include lines and coloured text boxes.

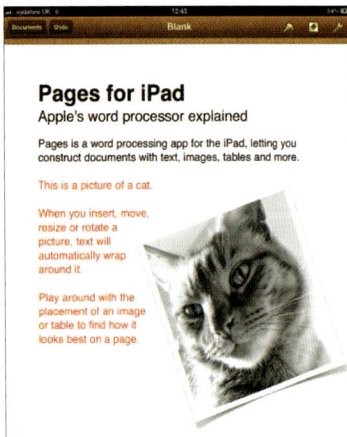

MOVING OBJECTS

6 When you select your chosen object it'll appear in your document. You can then drag it to where you want it and resize it using the blue dots. Text will wrap around objects automatically. You can adjust selected objects further by tapping the paintbrush icon – you may want to add a border to a photo, or move a text box in front of an image.

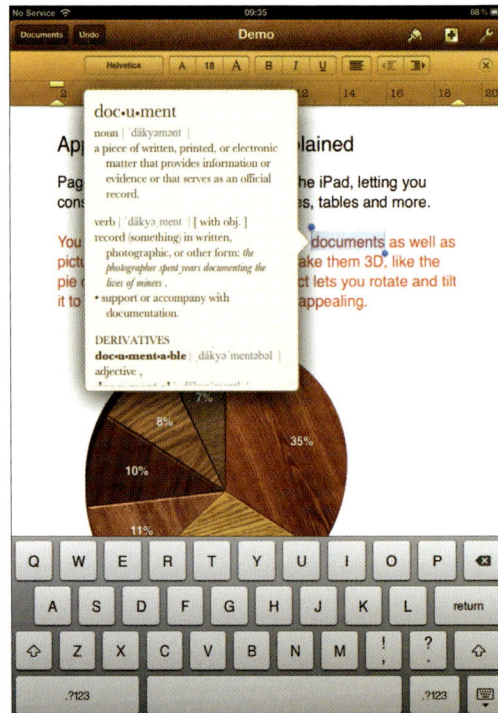

HANDY TIPS

7 You can check a word's definition by highlighting it with a double-tap, then choosing 'Define'. A dictionary entry will instantly pop up. You can also scroll speedily through multi-page documents using the Navigator: place a finger in the right margin of a page until it appears, then drag up and down to jump to any page.

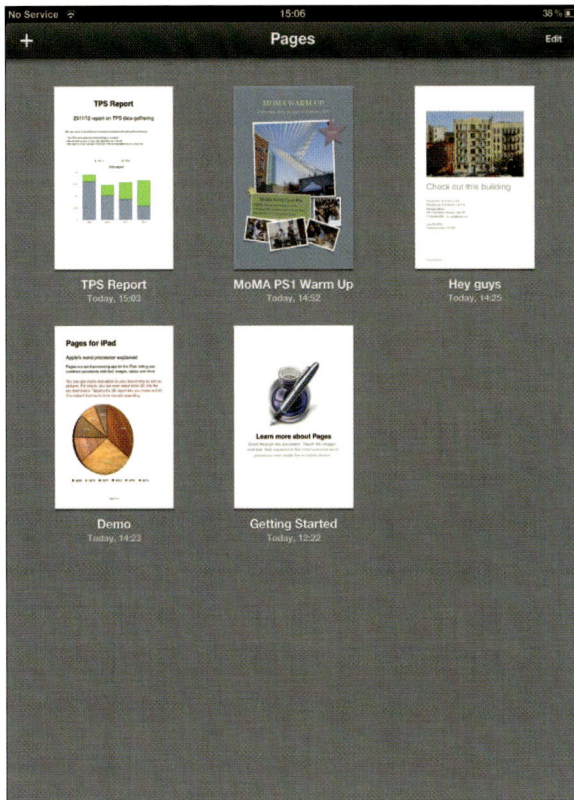

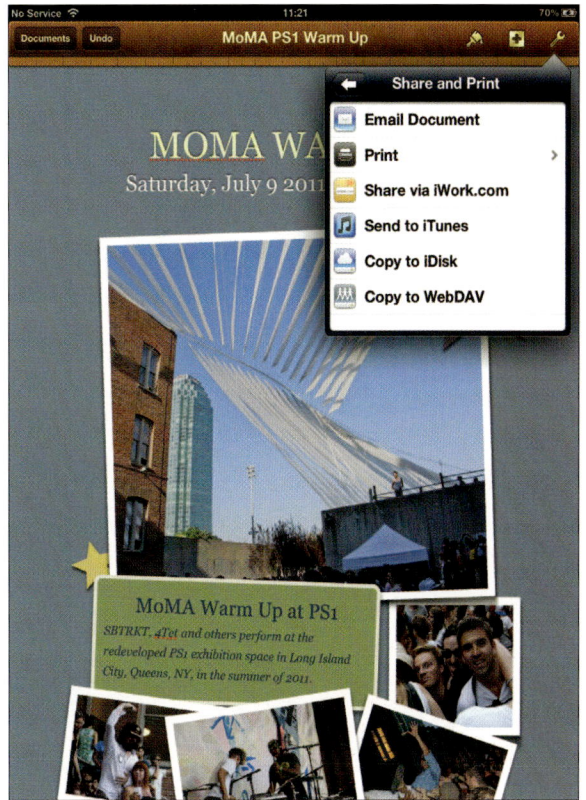

ORGANISING DOCUMENTS

8 Pages files are automatically saved into the Documents view (always accessible at the top left of the screen), and you can quickly share, duplicate or delete them here. To group documents into folders, hold your finger on a document until it 'jiggles', then drag it on top of another document.

SHARING YOUR PAGES

9 Tap the 'Tools' button (the spanner icon) at any time and select 'Share and Print'. This lets you email the document, print it, copy it to WebDAV or iDisk, share it to iWork.com (Apple's online document sharing service, currently in beta) or send it to your computer via iTunes.

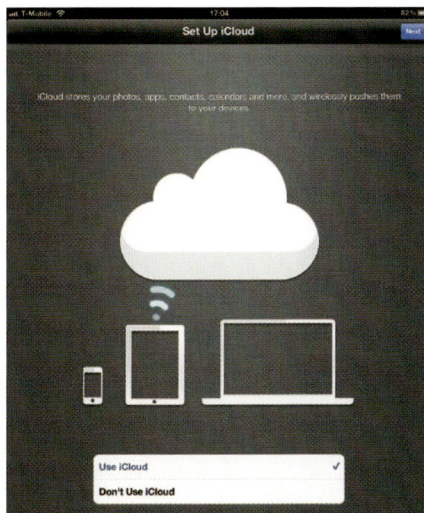

iCLOUD

10 Make sure you have an iCloud account if you own a Mac (running OS X Lion or better) and/or an iPhone or iPod Touch. This will automatically keep your Pages documents safely stored in the cloud, as well as accessible in their most up-to-date form on all your devices.

Watch TV shows and movies on your iPad

▶ The new iPad's fantastic Retina display makes it the perfect portable video player, and you can use iTunes to download movies and TV shows to the device's built-in memory. But that's just the tip of the iceberg for the iPad – thanks to a bevy of streaming services, it's easier than ever to watch your favourite films delivered directly from the cloud. We'll be looking at four of the iPad's most popular TV and movie streaming apps – BBC iPlayer, Netflix, LOVEFiLM and Sky Go. Read on, and we'll explain what they do and how to get the best out of them on your tablet.

VITAL INFO

We'll show you how to search for and stream TV shows and movies to your iPad – and you'll even get a few tips on finding recommendations for your future viewing.

What you need
Your iPad
Sky Go, BBC iPlayer, Netflix or LOVEFiLM apps (available from the App Store)

Time required
As much time as it takes to watch your favourite shows

WHAT IT DOES

1 Free to anyone with a Sky TV account, Sky Go offers iPad access to the TV content you already pay for: to get movies on your iPad, you'll need to subscribe to the Sky Movies package at home. It features both live TV and Anytime+ on-demand content.

Sky Go

REGISTERING YOUR IPAD

2 You'll need a Sky Go account to use the service, so head over to the Sky Go website and create one using your Sky ID information. You can register up to two devices per household (these include phones, laptops and games consoles).

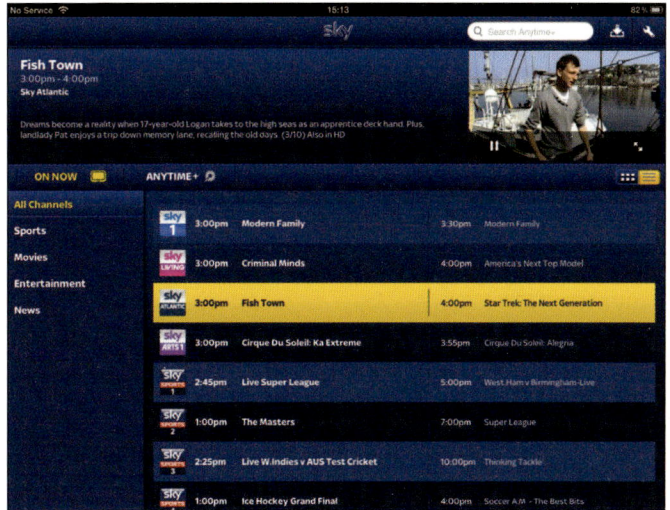

WATCHING LIVE TV

3 Sky Go's iPad app features 23 live TV channels, and you can see what's currently showing by tapping the home page's 'On Now' button to bring up a guide. Hitting one of the channels will display the current programme in the top right mini-viewer, which can then be expanded to fill the entire screen.

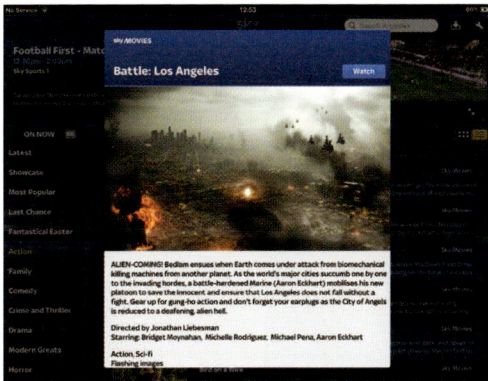

WATCHING ON-DEMAND CONTENT

4 Anytime+ on-demand content is available through the app, but unlike the console and PC versions of Sky Go, it's currently limited to movies – Sky has restrictions on what content can be accessed through a mobile device. There are over 600 films available to Sky Movie Pack subscribers: just hit the Anytime+ tab and browse by genre or popularity.

OUT AND ABOUT

5 Sky Go works over both WiFi and 3G, so you can use it when you're on the move if you have a fast enough connection. You can also pause an Anytime+ movie mid-play and have it resume later at the same point, which is very handy if you're constantly moving from place to place.

BBC iPlayer

WHAT IT DOES

1 The BBC iPlayer app gives you access to a huge range of 'catch-up' BBC TV and radio programmes, as well as live broadcasts. It's free and incredibly simple to use – making it an app that every iPad user should own. Note that it only works over WiFi, however, and won't let you download shows for offline viewing.

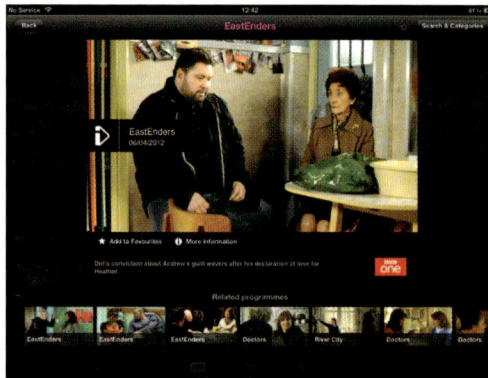

THE HOME SCREEN

2 The Home screen features three main tabs – Featured, Most Popular and For You – that present you with programming, while the buttons at the bottom toggle between TV, radio and Favourites. Selecting a programme lets you watch it or add it to your Favourites, and presents a selection of similar programming on a scrollable bar at the bottom.

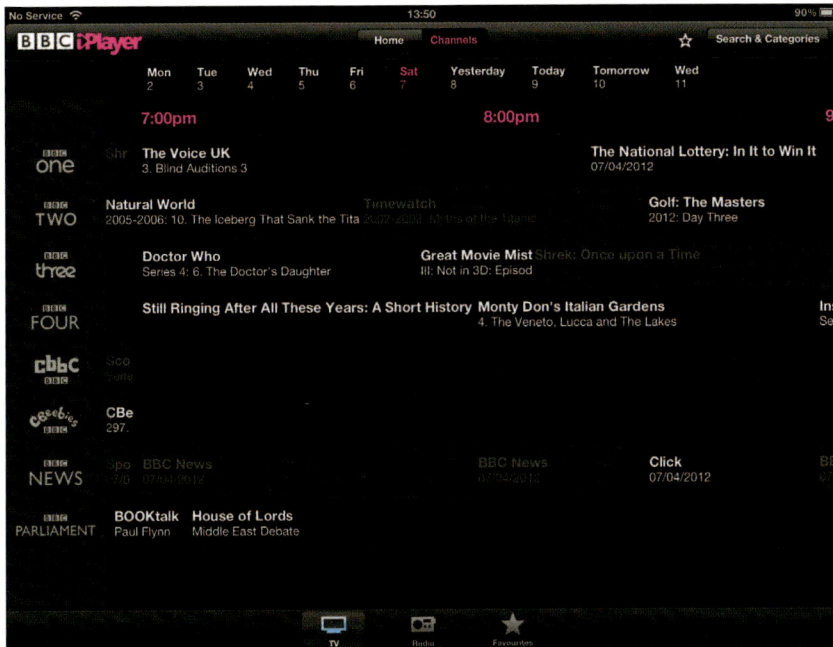

THE CHANNELS SCREEN

3 The Channels screen features a guide to what's currently being broadcast on BBC TV and radio. For many programmes, it gives you the option to tune in live. You can also go back to previous days (up to a week) and tap on highlighted shows to view them.

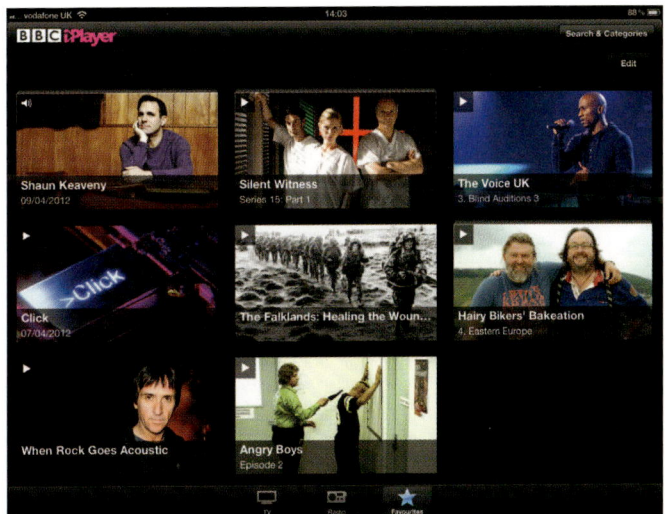

SEARCH & CATEGORIES

4 If you already know what you want to watch, hitting the Search & Categories button at the top right allows you to find it: just type it in to the box that appears. Alternatively, you can browse detailed programme categories until you find something you like the look of.

FAVOURITES

5 Tapping the star icon on programmes you like adds them to your Favourites list, allowing you to skip directly to them from the Home screen. Sadly, your iPad Favourites won't show up when you use iPlayer on your PS3, laptop or phone, due to the fact that you're not logged into a central account – something for the Beeb to add in the future, perhaps.

Netflix

WHAT IT DOES

1 Netflix offers its members unlimited access to movies and TV shows for £5.99 a month. iPad streaming is just one part of the service: content can also be accessed via your games console, smart TV, Apple TV, set-top box or computer. You can even start watching on one device and continue on another, right from where you left off!

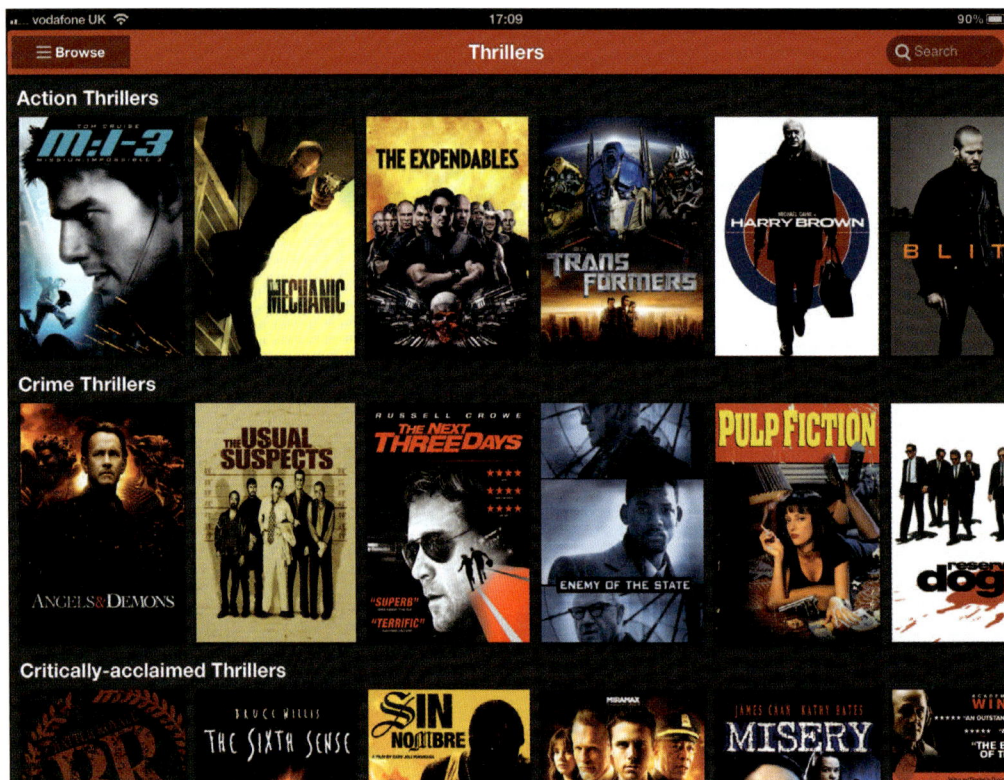

FINDING A FILM

2 The Netflix app's home screen features a selection of suggested movies and TV shows based on type ('Inspiring', 'mind-bending', 'violent', 'critically acclaimed' etc.), but you can search for a specific title using the box at the top right, or browse by genre using the button at the top left.

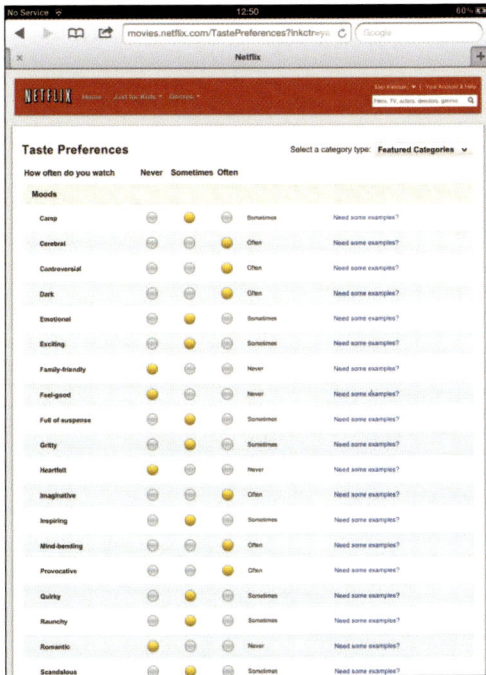

TAILOR CONTENT TO YOUR TASTES

3 There are over 6,000 movies and TV shows to watch on Netflix and they change every day, so setting your preferred type of movies and shows can help sharpen the app's suggestions. Head over to the Netflix website's 'Taste Preferences' page and rate the 'moods' or genres of films according to your tastes. This will ensure the app recommends the right kind of content as and when it appears on the service. The content choices will be important if you want to avoid certain movies or TV shows during family viewing sessions, although you can also password protect your account too.

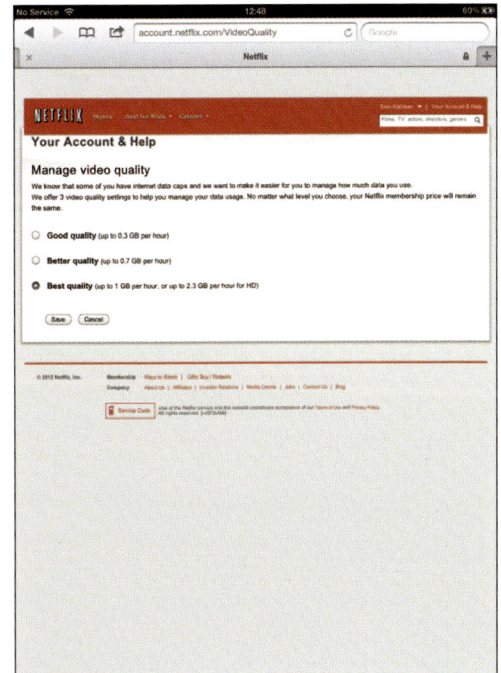

KEEPING IT SOCIAL

4 You can connect your Netflix and Facebook accounts, which will enable you to see what your friends have been watching – it's another way of getting recommendations. If you don't want to reveal your viewing habits to the world, just hit the 'Don't Share This' button at the top right when you start watching a film.

VIDEO QUALITY

5 If you have a download cap on your broadband or mobile data and you're worried about using it all up by streaming videos, you can lower the quality. At its lowest setting, Netflix will use up to 0.3GB of data per hour of viewing; at its highest, it'll eat up as much as 1GB.

LOVEFiLM Player

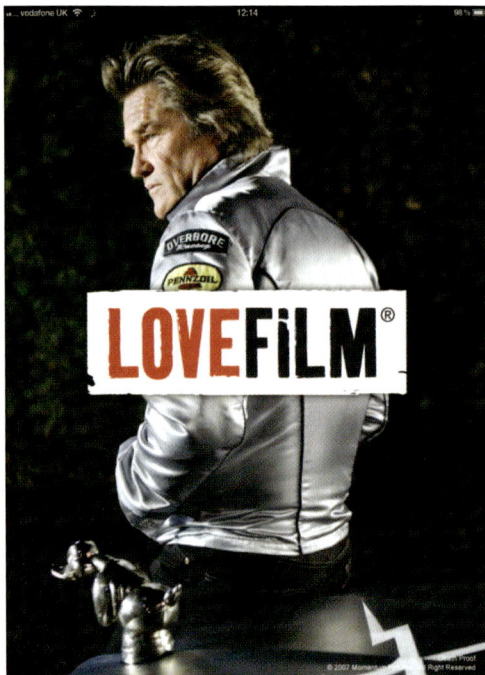

WHAT IT DOES

1 The Amazon-owned LOVEFiLM works in a similar way to Netflix, although it offers a largely different selection of TV and film content as the two services have deals with different studios. New users can sign up for a free 30-day trial, after which unlimited streaming is available for an introductory price of £4.99 a month.

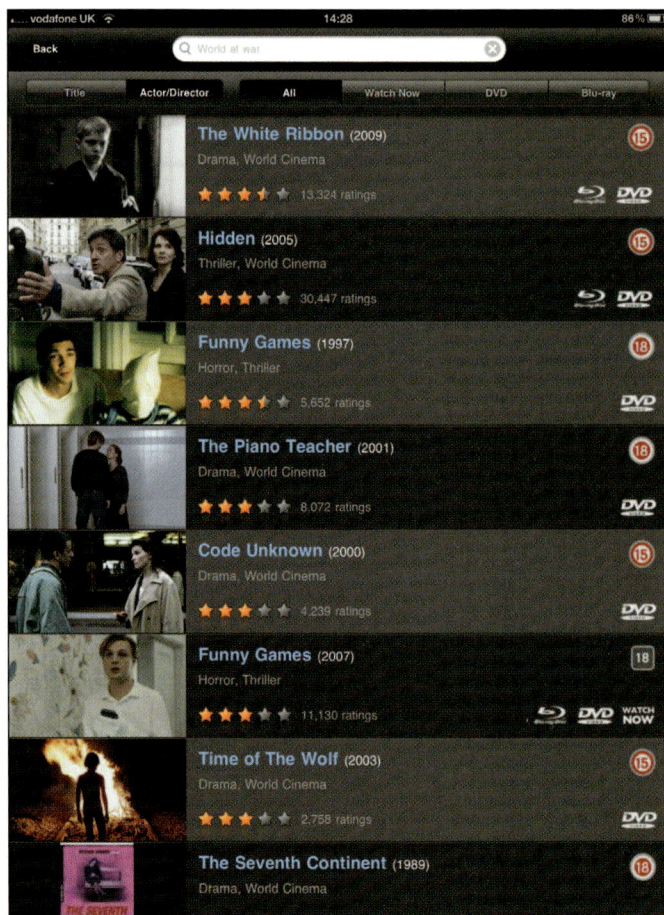

FINDING A FILM

2 The home screen makes it easy to select a movie or TV show. You can search for a specific film by typing in a title at the top right, or browse using the category tabs by genre, rating and popularity. LOVEFiLM also provides weekly recommendations, as well as collections, which bring thematically linked or otherwise related groups of videos together.

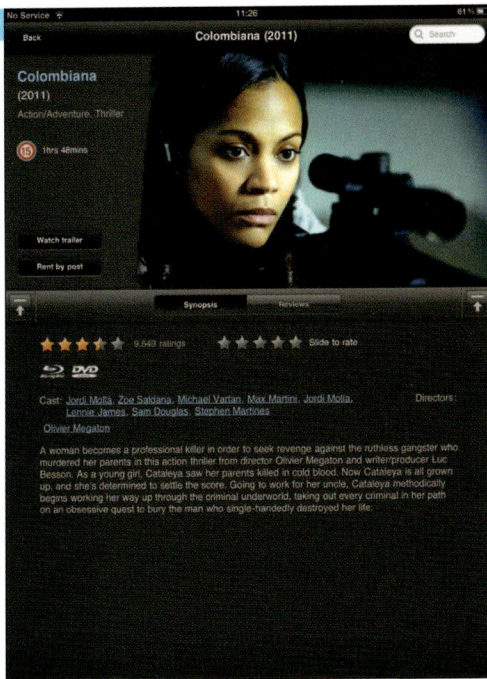

GETTING MORE INFO

3 Each film or show's screen provides a wealth of information, including running time and user-written reviews. You can also view a trailer for the movie, choose to rent it on DVD or Blu-ray by post (if you have the relevant subscription), and clicking on the names of stars or the director takes you to their other films.

LOVEFiLM vs Netflix

While seemingly similar, there are quite a few differences between these two rival on-demand services. LOVEFiLM lets you rent physical DVDs and Blu-ray discs as well as streaming, and generally offers better video quality (at least where the iPad is concerned). Netflix has a different selection of movies – which could be better or worse, depending on your tastes – and works over 3G.

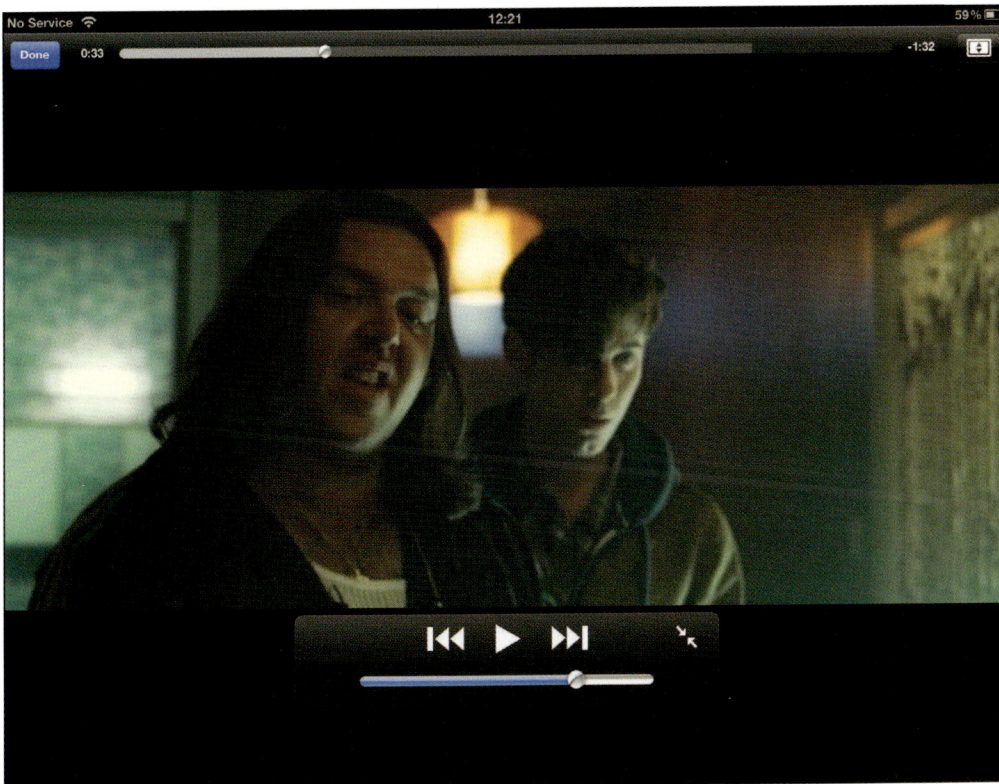

WATCHING MOVIES

4 LOVEFiLM lacks the 'start watching on one device, pick up from the same place on another' functionality of Netflix, but aside from that its movie playback is similar: you can pause, rewind and fast forward films, and 'scrub' through to a certain point using the usual Apple progress bar at the top.

Use your iPad as a second screen

▶ With many of us multi-tasking these days both at home and in the office, it's often useful to have some extra screen area at your disposal. Thanks to the Air Display app, you can transform your iPad into this all-important extra screen space.

Configuring your iPad to work as a second display for your desktop computer or laptop takes a matter of minutes. The great thing is that you can control standard Mac windows and dialog boxes using the touchscreen, and the app is perfect for anyone who has a busy life – or just a tendency to have lots of active windows and to find that their workspace is cramped and cluttered when working with only one screen.

Air Display is fine for day-to-day tasks, although it might struggle with more challenging work such as handling video footage – but it's still an invaluable desktop aid.

VITAL INFO

This tutorial will take you through the steps involved in turning your iPad into a wireless display that allows you to expand your normal computer desktop onto a secondary working area. All you need is the app, an iPad with iOS 3.2 or later, another computer and wireless connectivity.

What you need
Your iPad
Air Display app (£6.99)
Air Display desktop app (free)

Time required
15 minutes

The set-up process

Air Display is quick to configure on your iPad, thanks to the clear interface that appears once downloaded. Each tab contains a step in the process.

Windows or Mac

Toggle between the set-up process for Mac or PC set-up using these simple icons.

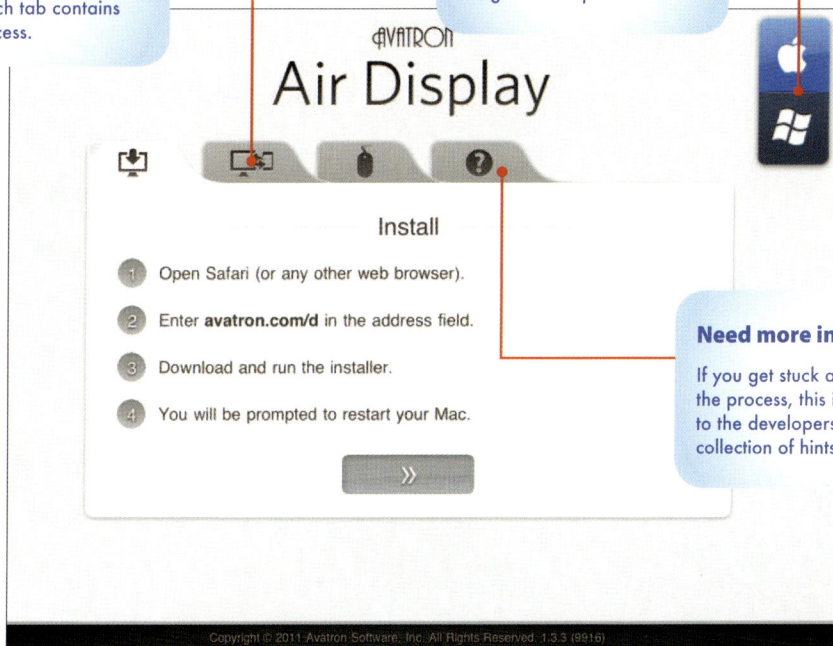

AVATRON

Air Display

Install

1. Open Safari (or any other web browser).
2. Enter **avatron.com/d** in the address field.
3. Download and run the installer.
4. You will be prompted to restart your Mac.

»

Need more info?

If you get stuck at any point in the process, this icon takes you to the developers' website for a collection of hints and tips.

EXPERT TIP

Air Display is happy working in either landscape or portrait configurations. Simply rotate your iPad as normal and the working area will respond accordingly. It works with both Mac and Windows computers for the ultimate in flexibility.

Turn on

To get Air Display to work, you have to download an app from the Avatron website (http://avatron.com/d). This installs an app that lets you turn the Air Display function on and off.

Air Display

Show All

Air Display

Connect   Settings

Status: **On**

Air Display is currently on. Choose a device below to be a virtual screen.

Device ✓ No device selected
          Tim's iPad

When you select a device, the screen will go blue as the system adds a new screen.

OFF   ON

1.3.3 (9987)

☑ Show Air Display in menu bar

System Preferences

Alternatively, open this window through 'System Preferences', which will then allow you to fine-tune any of Air Display's settings.

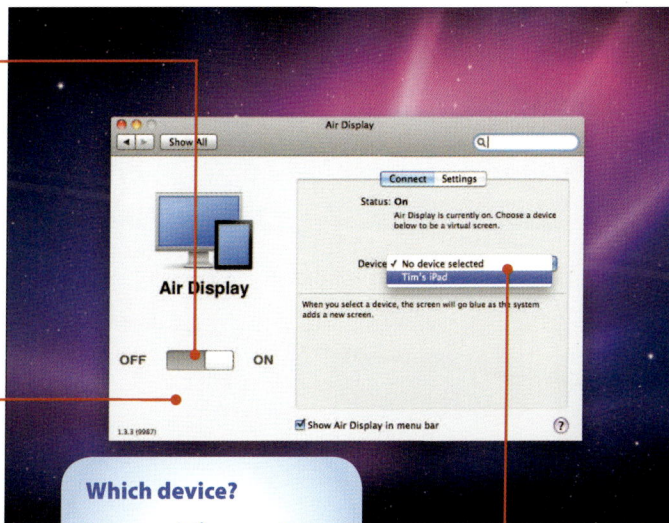

Which device?

You can pair the computer with your iPad simply by selecting it with the device that appear in the menu. Add more devices if you need to.

Step-by-step guide ⟫

Be more productive

By expanding your working area, Air Display allows you to get much more done. It gives you the ability to turn your iPad into a secondary monitor that will run happily alongside your normal desktop Mac or PC. And configuration couldn't be simpler – here's how it's done…

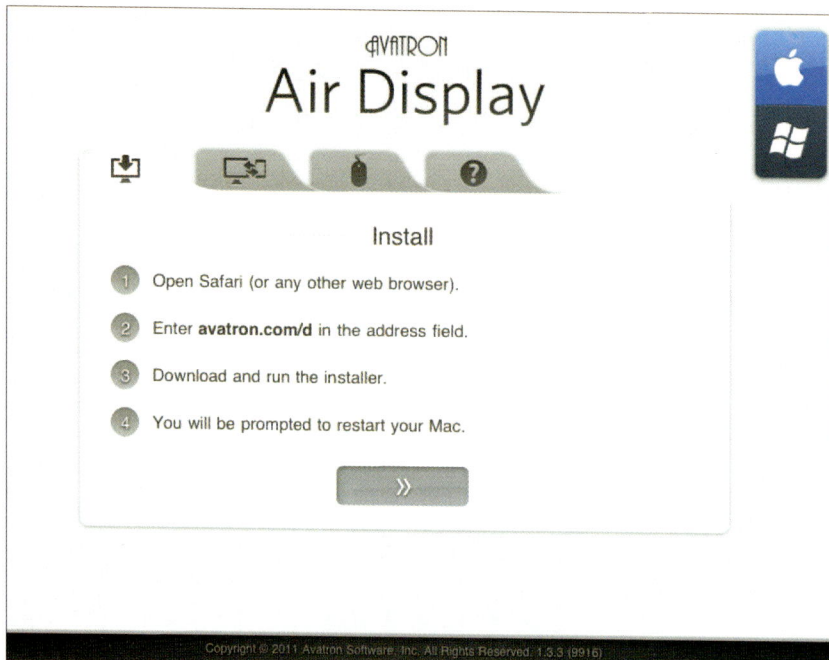

NEED TO KNOW
Resolutions

Resolutions:

800 × 500
800 × 600
800 × 600 (stretched)
1024 × 640
1024 × 768

Air Display allows you to select different resolutions for the screen that you're using by dipping into the 'Display' preferences. Access this from the top right-hand menu next to Time Machine.

1 After downloading Air Display to your iPad, follow the straightforward instructions to configure the software. You'll see this four-tab dialog window. Go to the web address avatron.com/d to download the software for the machine you're pairing it with.

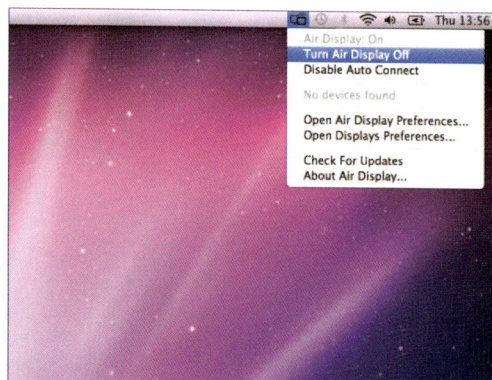

2 Click the version you wish to install and follow the instructions. This will require you to restart your machine. Once installed, an icon will appear in the top-right of the screen if you are on a Mac, or in the bottom-right on a PC.

3 Air Display can be controlled using the menu that will appear at the top right of your computer screen. This allows you to switch it on or off on the computer that you installed it on, and access the 'Preferences' area for pairing to your iPad.

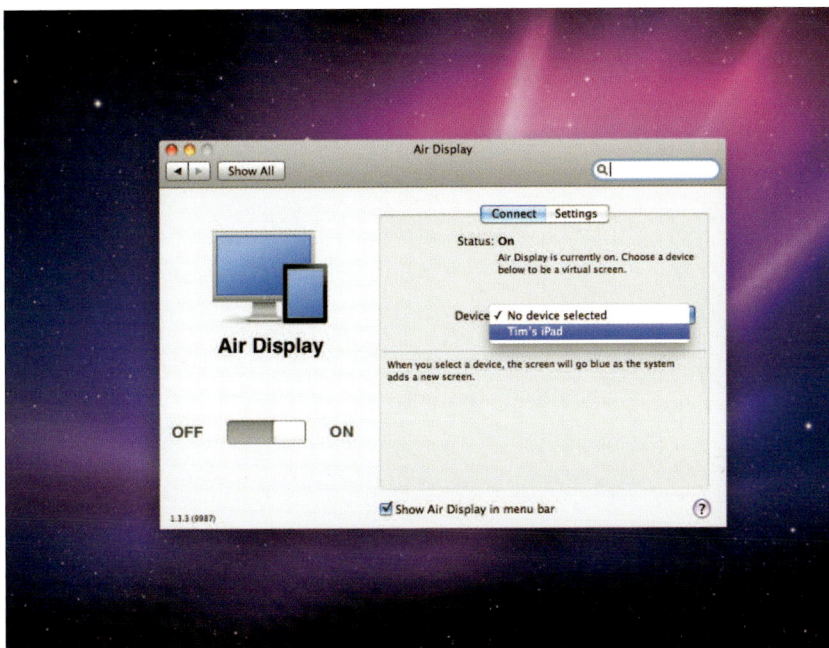

WANT MORE?
Print Sharing

Print sharing apps allow you to access, edit and print digital documents across a variety of devices and platforms, including different operating systems. One good example, the imaginatively titled Print Sharing (£1.79) comes from the same developer as Air Display.

4 The 'Preferences' window allows you to select your iPad from this drop-down list. Be sure that you have WiFi enabled and that both devices are using the same connection.

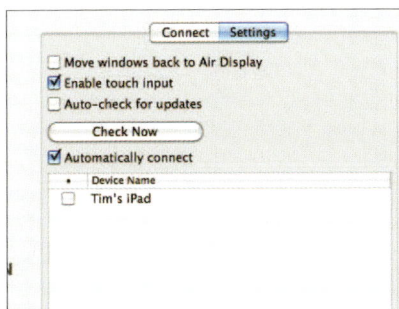

5 Click on the 'Settings' tab in the dialog box in order to fine-tune Air Display's settings, for example by choosing to enable touch input, or by automatically enabling Air Display when you connect your iPad to your computer.

6 Find out how to use the dual-screen controls and get handy tips for better performance by watching the 'Mouse' video in the Air Display app on your iPad.

iPad the third generation

We review the new iPad and see what lies beneath the new bonnet...

What do you want to use your iPad for? And which model should you buy? If you already have an iPad 2, do you really need to upgrade?

Last year, when Apple released the iPad 2, the original iPad was quickly taken off the market. This year, though, Apple has kept the iPad 2 on sale alongside the 'new iPad'. There's no iPad 3 name convention and Apple simply refers to the third-generation iPad as the 'new iPad'.

Since one is called iPad and the other iPad 2, it's last year's model that sounds like it's the newer product, but, ultimately, this is Apple's way of saying the iPad is here to stay and probably won't have numbers attached to future releases in a similar way to the iPod and MacBook range of laptops.

iPad 2 is now only available in its lowest capacity 16GB model, and either WiFi or WiFi + 3G connectivity options. The price has also been reduced by £70 since it launched last spring to a Samsung-worrying £329. At this new price point, iPad 2 remains the best-in-class tablet and throws doubt on previously cheaper Android rivals like the Samsung Galaxy Tab 10.1 and Motorola Xoom 2.

Apple has done a clever thing here: other companies might have devised a separate low-end model. Apart from the costs of developing another gadget, it would probably end up with cheaper components or a less upscale feel. Apple's iPad 2 remains classy and it has cost Apple nothing to deliver it, apart from altering the price tag.

For £329, you can buy a beautifully thin, aluminium and glass tablet that offers access to 200,000 dedicated apps, with an increasing concentration on landmark business and design apps alongside games. Even if you count apps that work on both phone and tablet, as Android does, Apple is still out in front, with over half a million titles. It has a fast processor, attractive screen and an interface that has still to be bettered in terms of usability.

Perhaps more noticeable than the resolution increase is the colour saturation

New tablet hero?

The iPad 2 is an impressive piece of kit, and at its new price will surely win many doubters over – a great tablet for a little more than £300 is persuasive. Okay, you may be wondering, are we suggesting it's not worth spending more for this year's model? Or, if you have an iPad 2 already, should you upgrade?

Well, if you want the lightest, thinnest iPad, you shouldn't. The new model is fatter and heavier. You really can't see the difference easily – it's only 0.6mm thicker. But you can feel that the new iPad is heavier by 61g. Even so, it's still lighter than the first iPad. But the lower weight is the only way the iPad 2 beats the new model. Of course, the screen is the headline upgrade on the new edition. The first two iPads had excellent displays but the new Retina Display is both spectacular and understated.

Put the old and new iPads side by side and you can see the difference, but it's clearest when you're using apps that have been updated for the new screen. Books are a real stand-out. Reading text from the iPad 2 was always average, but when once you've grown accustomed to using the new model, you'll suddenly see jagged edges on letters and slightly blurred lines if you return to its predecessor.

On the new iPad, it's much closer to the ideal: a printed piece of paper with crisp, super-sharp text. The Retina display grows on you with time, and as more apps are Retina-optimised, it will grow even clearer. Perhaps more noticeable than the resolution is the increase in colour saturation, up by over 40 per cent, according to Apple. This means it's bright, vivid and colourful, while avoiding the over-saturated pitfalls some AMOLED screens reveal.

The processor has been improved to manage all these extra pixels effectively. The A5X chip is essentially the same A5 processor as on the iPad 2, though with a greatly enhanced quad-core graphics processor. It doesn't make the new iPad more responsive, but it keeps everything on screen smooth and glitch-free. You'll notice the difference in games, video and photo editing. It's the upgrade Apple needed to combat Nvidia's Tegra 3 chip, which has been appearing in new Android tablets since late last year.

Video, storage and networks

Video looks great on the iPad 2, but if you download a movie from iTunes that's in 1080p HD on to the new iPad, the difference is exceptionally clear. Suddenly it's possible to have a truly high-definition 9.7in screen. Remember, the new iPad's display has more pixels in it ⟩⟩⟩

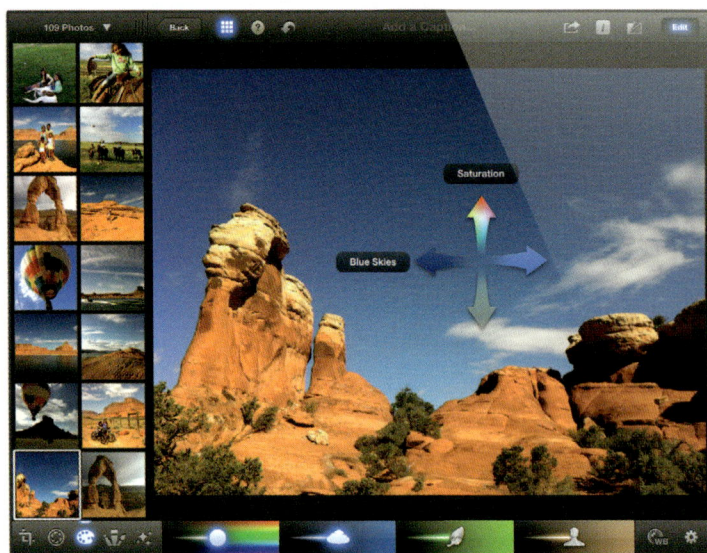

than a 55in Full HD TV. You won't be disappointed by video on the iPad 2, but here it's unbelievably sharp. For some, it will be difficult to go back to a lower resolution screen – either on a tablet or a desktop computer. It's also going to make the imperfections in older HD TVs look more obvious too. Motion tracking, detail and colour balance are all best in class, and instantly set a new benchmark for tablets.

With great resolution comes great file sizes, however. A 1080p HD movie can take up over 4GB of space, and if your broadband tariff has a cap you could bust that quickly. It also means the file takes longer to download and – most important of all – you'll fill your iPad's storage very quickly. True, you're more likely to rent a movie on the tablet rather than buy, but you still need the space for that rental

DICTATION: The best bit of Siri is featured on the new iPad but you'll need a quiet environment and good WiFi to use it properly

period. Suddenly, the 32GB and 64GB capacities seem more essential than on the iPad 2.

We downloaded episodes of Homeland and The River in HD which offered viewing quality unmatched by any mobile device, full stop. Again, the storage space is an issue – each episode weighs in at 1.4GB which means you couldn't download a full, 23-episode TV series on the entry-level 16GB iPad.

Of course, there's iCloud and the brilliant ability to stream to a £99 Apple TV, viewing any purchases on your TV. Film fans are going to love the new iPad – but just remember the benefits of the storage space your iPhone offers for music, and then consider that the entry-level iPad holds just a few HD films at a time, without taking into account apps and music. Apple is resolute in avoiding MicroSD card inputs that could double the size of available memory very cheaply, and it's one of the major issues we have with the next-generation tablet. As games, apps and movies get bigger and better, users need more storage. The 32GB WiFi version costs £479, while the 64GB WiFi model costs £559.

In terms of 4G versions, you can add £100 to each of those prices for easy internet (almost) everywhere with a PAYG SIM. We used a T-Mobile SIM and found performance great, though the added extras of the '4G' iPad involve 4G skills (alongside UK 3G functions), which will only be of use when you take the iPad abroad and join a 4G LTE network. The

■■ We found that the new iPad became hot during intensive use in a way that previous models didn't ■■

4G iPad supports HSPA, HSPA+ and DC-HSDPA.

Camera action

If you're a keen photographer, you'll know how disappointing the camera on the iPad 2 could be. To be fair, it was optimised for video, so only needed a low-resolution sensor for shooting video in HD. The new iPad's camera is hugely improved. It handles 1080p video recording, instead of 720p as before. And now it has a 5MP stills sensor, similar to that of the iPhone 4.

There's no flash, but a combination of complex lens construction and a backside illuminated sensor – where the wiring and other hardware is kept out of the way of the sensor – mean that it's efficient at making the most of the light available. There are extras the iPad 2 lacked too, such as image stabilisation when you're shooting video. The iPad version of iPhoto makes the most of the new camera, offering montages, comparison shots and intelligent photo

nips and tucks in seconds. Choose a montage of holiday pics and you can drag in date and weather icons that read the meta-data for the holiday snaps and go online to magically present you with the date and temperature of your time abroad. Another click exports the data-rich gallery and allows you to share it with friends and family. It might not sound like much, but it's arguably a family-friendly way of presenting photos that makes the traditional album or email stream of photos look old-fashioned. Expect to see the adverts soon, replacing the family FaceTime shorts.

If you're a keen photographer with an SLR camera, the new iPad is now significantly better for previewing your work on while you're on the go. The £25 Camera Connect Kit is essentially a small card reader for standard SD Card and USB sticks. Importing photos is fast but, again, it's the new Retina screen that produces stand-out results, far superior to the preview screens of high-end cameras or laptops. Interestingly, after less than an hour importing and editing 15-megapixel JPEG files, we found the new iPad became hot in a way that previous models hadn't. We used the 32GB and 64GB 4G versions, and found

the same issue with both. The enhanced A5X processor is great, of course, and heat is a problem that has plagued many laptops. The big difference is that the iPad has never used an internal fan and while not prohibitive, the heat generated is a minor blip within the traditionally flawless Apple user experience.

Siri calling?

Users of the iPhone 4S can use the voice control functions offered by Siri, which has met with a mixed reception – at least in the UK. Siri doesn't feature on the new iPad (or the iPad 2), but the best part of the program, Dictation, is included. This means that now every keyboard has a microphone icon next to the space bar. One tap and it'll transcribe what you say. Note that you need a decent internet connection and ideally to be in a quiet environment for best results. You won't be able to quietly speak into a headset in a busy Starbucks.

Dictation is very well executed, though iPad 2 users needn't upgrade for it. They can enjoy similar effects from excellent apps like Vlingo and Dragon Dictation. Audio transcription is just as good using these apps, though they make it a little less simple to paste the words into an email or text message. The connectivity you need for dictation and other features has been greatly enhanced for the new iPad, compared to the iPad 2. The more expensive model is billed as 'WiFi + 4G', and though that's true in the US, it »»

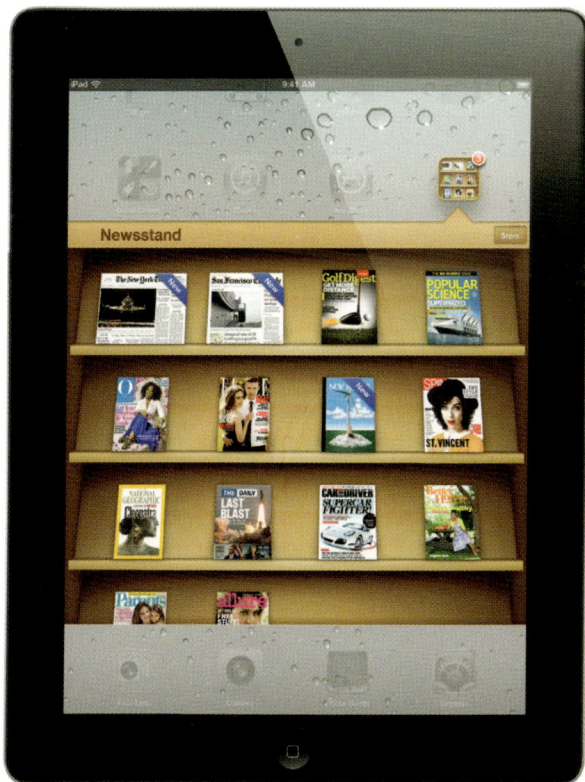

doesn't apply here in the UK where there aren't any 4G networks just yet. When they eventually arrive, they won't be compatible with the frequencies the new iPad can reach either.

Still, the new iPad can access HSPA+ and DC-HSDPA, the fastest 3G networks currently being rolled out in the UK. As these become more widespread it will mean download speeds of up to 42Mbps. The biggest issue when considering a 4G iPad for £100 more than the standard WiFi version is that many portable WiFi hot-spot devices are now around £30 with competitive PAYG cards. But if pure in-built convenience and internet access anywhere are paramount, the 4G version is perfect, especially if you regularly venture out of places with freely available WiFi.

Games and apps

Apple is keen to stress that the A5X processor benefits gamers, and the hero games that Apple chose to demo the new iPad with at launch were Infinity Blade and Sky Gamblers: Air Supremacy, both of which are optimised for the new tablet. While the improvements are welcome, they don't deliver the huge leap in performance that a new games console brings (see Nintendo DS vs 3DS or PSP vs PlayStation Vita), if only because there aren't enough new iPad-enhanced games just yet – but this will change. Apple has made no secret that it intends to grow the games available and go after big developers so that the next big game is an iPad exclusive. Mass Effect Infiltrator

at just £4.99 is a sign of things to come.

Apps are a different matter, and the new iPad-exclusive iPhoto is a revelation. Brushes, effects and clever tweaks bring the app into junior Photoshop territory. If you've used the entry-level Photoshop Elements you'll be impressed. Then there's the price: iPhoto is just £2.99, essential for all new iPad owners.

Likewise, Apple's own version of Word, called Pages, is easy to use and showcases the Retina screen again. Updates to Garage Band and iMovie prioritise the screen too – use them alongside the iPad 2 versions and the difference is easy to spot.

Consumer choices

Apple has made it hard to resist an iPad if you're in the market for a tablet – the £329 iPad 2 instantly threatens any Android tablet in the same price bracket and the new iPad is simply the iPad update Apple fans wanted – a better screen and more power for bigger, better apps. We've talked about the Retina display as the main stand-out factor of the new iPad but it's the new apps that will win the hearts of the public. Simply put, the new iPad is a great upgrade for iPad fans but, as the the app store offers more and more incentives, it will become a truly essential purchase. Android may be taking the fight to Apple in the smartphone market, but in the world of tablets, it's possible that Apple has delivered the two-pronged (iPad 2, new iPad) assault on Android to end the 2012 tablet war early...

The biggest issue when considering a 4G iPad is that many portable WiFi hotspot devices cost just £30

SCREEN:
9.7 inch Retina display with a 2048 x 1536 pixel display. You haven't seen a screen this sharp anywhere - fact

THE VERDICT:
Beats AMOLED rivals and iPad 2 hands down. We don't expect to see a better screen for some time...

BODY:
The same Apple build quality, but 61g heavier

THE VERDICT:
The luxury Apple design looks great, though the Smart Cover is as essential as ever. The extra weight is a disappointing backwards step, however.

PERFORMANCE:
A5X chip, with quad-core graphics power

THE VERDICT:
If you're a gamer, you'll instantly upgrade. The A5X chip has the power that makes it worth throwing games to your HDTV. Watch out Sony and Microsoft...

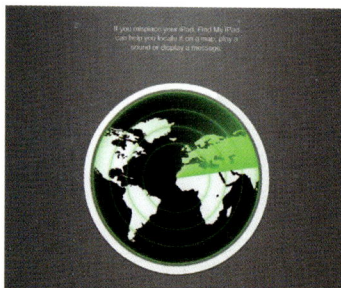

CONNECTIVITY:
4G and WiFi options and everything you could hope for

THE VERDICT:
A landmark tablet for connectivity if you live in America and can use 4G, but still an impressive WiFi and 3G device for UK users – iOS 5.1 makes connecting easy.